FROM

YOU ARE AMAZING!

GET AROUND GOOD PEOPLE THAT
WILL SUPPORT YOU!

YOU HAVE WHAT IT TAKES!

KEEP CLIMBING!

PUT IN THE WORK!

DREAM B.I.G.!

STAY THE COURSE!

WIN FOR YOU AND YOUR FAMILY!

NEVER GIVE UP!

.

EVERYDAY YOU GET UP AND RUN TOWARDS THE BATTLE,

WHILE OTHERS ARE RUNNING FROM IT.

YOU ARE THE TRUE HEROES.

WHAT OTHERS ARE SAYING ABOUT 'FROM THE PIT TO THE PALACE'...

"A DELIGHTFUL AND EMPOWERING READ. THIS BOOK ENCOURAGES YOU TO CHASE YOUR DREAMS FEARLESSLY AND EMBRACE THE JOURNEY OF SELF-DISCOVERY. TOM'S SINCERITY POURS OUT OF THIS BOOK WITH EVERY WORD, EVERY PAGE. I HAVE HAD THE HONOR OF KNOWING TOM THROUGH HIS JOURNEY OVER THE PAST 40+ YEARS AND I WILL HAPPILY SHARE THIS BOOK WITH MUCH PRIDE. I AM HUMBLED TO STILL BE A PART OF HIS LIFE."

SAM CONSTANTINO

"AS AN EDUCATOR, I'VE TAUGHT HIGH SCHOOL AND MIDDLE SCHOOL FOR 23 YEARS AND TOM VARANO'S BOOK IS AN EMPOWERING READ FOR MIDDLE AND HIGH SCHOOL STUDENTS, AS THIS BOOK CELEBRATES INDIVIDUALITY AND ENCOURAGES YOUNG MINDS TO EMBRACE THEIR UNIQUE STRENGTHS AND DREAMS. IT IS A LIGHTHOUSE WHOSE BEACON REACHES AND SOOTHES THEIR DOUBTS, AND THEY ARE TO CAPTAIN THEIR OWN SHIP, EVEN IN THE STORMIEST OF SEAS."

MAJOR WILLIAM MIMIAGA USMC (RET)

"I STARTED MARKING YELLOW PASSAGES I LIKED, BUT I GAVE UP BECAUSE EVERYTHING WAS YELLOW. VERY FEW BOOKS HAVE TOUCHED ME IN THE WAY TOM'S BOOK HAS. UNBELIEVABLE, HOW MUCH I RECOGNIZE MYSELF IN IT, AS I THINK WE ALL WILL RECOGNIZE OURSELVES IN IT. THE BOOK IS AN EYE OPENER, MAKING ME REALIZE IT IS NEVER TOO LATE TO CHANGE, TO FOLLOW MY DREAMS. TOM, MY FRIEND, THANKS FOR WRITING THE BOOK, YOU MADE ME A CHANGED MAN."

AAD DE LANGE

"TOM'S BOOK REITERATES THE IMPORTANCE OF KINDNESS AND HARD WORK FOR LIVING A HAPPY, HEALTHY, SUCCESSFUL LIFE."

**TIMOTHY JENNY
SUPERINTENDENT REMSEN CENTRAL SCHOOL**

"HAVING HAD THE PLEASURE OF KNOWING TOM WHILE HE WAS IN HIGH SCHOOL ALLOWS ME TO SAY WITH 100% CERTAINTY THAT OFTENTIMES IT'S IMPOSSIBLE TO KNOW AND TO UNDERSTAND ALL THE BAGGAGE THAT PEOPLE CARRY AROUND WITH THEM. A SEEMINGLY "NORMAL" KID, A FRIEND TO MANY, AN ATHLETE, A PERSON OF FAITH WHO APPEARS TO HAVE IT ALL TOGETHER STILL HAS A STORY TO TELL. WE CAN NEVER JUDGE A BOOK BY ITS COVER. WE NEED TO PROVIDE THE ENVIRONMENT AND THE OPPORTUNITIES FOR KIDS TO FEEL COMFORTABLE SHARING THESE STORIES. THOSE CONVERSATIONS, COURAGEOUS AT TIMES, CAN BE LIBERATING. TO KNOW THAT YOU'RE NOT ALONE AND THAT PEOPLE CARE TO LISTEN CAN BEGIN THE JOURNEY OF HEALING. I WOULD ENCOURAGE ADULTS TO PICK UP THIS BOOK, READ IT AND THEN CHALLENGE THEMSELVES TO LOOK AT PEOPLE, ESPECIALLY KIDS AND YOUNG ADULTS A LITTLE DIFFERENTLY, TO LOOK AT THEM AND TO UNDERSTAND THAT THERE IS A LOT THAT DOESN'T MEET THE EYE. DON'T JUDGE, JUST SHOW THEM THAT YOU UNDERSTAND."

ROCCO MIGLIORI
SUPERINTENDENT WESTMORELAND CSD

"IF YOU'RE LOOKING FOR A BOOK THAT WILL UPLIFT YOUR SOUL AND IGNITE YOUR PASSION, LOOK NO FURTHER. THIS INSPIRING READ WILL AWAKEN YOUR INNER FIRE AND EMPOWER YOU TO CHASE YOUR DREAMS FEARLESSLY."

MOSONGO OSONG
CEO/FOUNDER, CATHOLICBRAIN, INC

"TOM BRINGS THE SAME POSITIVE ENERGY HE SHARES DURING A PRESENTATION TO HIS WRITING. FROM THE PIT TO THE PALACE IS AN INSPIRING JOURNEY OF SELF-DISCOVERY ALL SHOULD TAKE. A REMINDER TO RELENTLESSLY CHASE YOUR DREAMS, FEARLESSLY EMBRACE YOUR UNIQUENESS AND TO THOUGHTFULLY CULTIVATE AND USE YOUR VOICE TO EMPOWER OTHERS."

JILL WICKJULIA WICK
SCHOOL COUNSELOR 4-8 DERUYTER CSD

"I FOUND MYSELF NODDING, SMILING, AND EVEN SHEDDING A TEAR WHILE READING THIS REMARKABLE BOOK. IT'S A TESTAMENT TO THE INDOMITABLE HUMAN SPIRIT AND THE POWER OF POSITIVITY. HIGHLY RECOMMENDED!"

CASS WELDON
ADVANCE AUTO PARTS

"STOP WHATEVER YOU ARE DOING AND READ THIS BOOK NOW. IT WILL SHIFT YOUR PERSPECTIVE, STRENGTHEN YOUR FAITH, AND FILL YOU WITH THE COURAGE TO FACE EACH NEW CHALLENGE WITH GRACE."

BARB ALLEN
CO-FOUNDER OF GREAT AMERICAN SYNDICATE, AUTHOR, GOLD STAR WIFE

"THIS BOOK WAS TRULY INSPIRING AND ALLOWED ME TO REFLECT ON WHAT IS IMPORTANT IN LIFE; COMPASSION, DETERMINATION TO MAKE CHANGE NOT ONLY IN MY LIFE BUT OTHERS AS WELL, HOPE AND LOVE. PASS IT ON. OUR SENSES BECOME MORE VIVID WHEN WE EXPERIENCE THE HAND OF GOD."

DARCY BRODMERKEL, M.ED., CAADC
DIRECTOR OF NEW STUDENT & FAMILY PROGRAMS
MISERICORDIA UNIVERSITY

"THIS BOOK DELIVERS A POWERFUL PUNCH OF POSITIVITY AND INSPIRATION, LIGHTING UP OUR PATH TO A BRIGHTER LIFE. THROUGH RELATABLE STORIES AND PRACTICAL ADVICE, IT'S A GUIDE THAT FUELS OUR INNER FIRE AND EQUIPS US TO CONQUER CHALLENGES WITH CONFIDENCE."

ERIC KONOVALOV

"TOM'S BOOK HAS CAPTURED THE ESSENCE OF POSITIVE THINKING. IT ENCOURAGES YOU TO DREAM AND BELIEVE IN YOURSELF AND THOSE WHO LOVE YOU AND THOSE YOU LOVE. TOM'S MESSAGE IS SO INSPIRING. I URGE THOSE WHO HAVE DOUBTS ABOUT THEIR FUTURE TO READ THIS BOOK."

TOM CLARK
FOUNDER OF ADIRONDACK BANK
MCDONALD'S OWNER OPERATOR

"GOD IS A WILD MAN...SHOULD YOU ENCOUNTER HIM...HANG

ON FOR DEAR LIFE-OR LET GO FOR DEAR LIFE IS A BETTER

WAY TO SAY IT."

-RICH MULLINS

"WRITTEN FOR THOSE THAT CONTINUE TO PUT FORTH THE COURAGE AND EFFORT TO KEEP CLIMBING THROUGH THE TRIALS OF LIFE."

-TOM VARANO

FROM THE PIT TO THE PALACE

STORIES OF OVERCOMING THE ODDS

Tom Varano

Copyright © 2023 Tom Varano

Illustrations Copyright © 2023 Tom Varano

Design Tom Varano

All rights reserved.

ISBN:9798856057545

Printed in the United States of America

First Printing August 2023

FROM THE PIT TO THE PALACE

STORIES OF OVERCOMING THE ODDS

SPECIAL THANKS TO:

DAVE BROWN & BARB ALLEN

KAREN VARANO

DIANE VOIRIN

TONY MAGLIO

SCOTT ROYCE

JENNIFER KELTNER

CHRIS MULDOON

ERIC LeFEVRE

MIKE & MARIE EGNOTO

HUSTON & JORDYNN SMITH

TOM & LAURA PASTERNAK

PATRICK & TISHA FRANCESCONE

DAN & NANCY BRECKENRIDGE

CHET & BARB LUSZCZYNSKI

DAVID & EMMY LILHOLT

ERIK & KRISTEN SHAW

WIL & MARILYN DAVIS

PAUL & TRACI RANKIN

RICH NIKODEM

TIM MOYER

TABLE OF CONTENTS

DEDICATION

As God's fingerprints are all over my life, in all my stories-
the ups and downs, so are the fingerprints of my daughters,
many family members, close friends, my business team, my
agents and my clients. You are the
people that have encouraged me. Believed in me.

This book is dedicated to you.

SPECIAL DEDICATION

I personally believe we each have angels walking this earth
specifically assigned to us. Heavenly sent trying to guide us,
helping us to find our North Star, the true mission that we
were created for. I've been fortunate enough to have many
angels cross my path, and for each one of them,
I'm beyond grateful.

Here some, but not all, I'd like to mention:

My Dad
Fr. Philip Hearn
Lee and Sue Idleman
Dick and Maureen Sullivan
My Mom

DIAMOND DEDICATION

And yes, I hear you as you're reading, saying,
"Man this guy has a lot of dedications."
Fortunately for me, you're right.

At this point, if we were drinking wine, I'd be holding up a
glass of the finest Cabernet Sauvignon saying...

...To my wife Karen...

My best friend. My greatest gift. My beauty. My diamond,
who found me in the rough (in the pit) and who is daily
working on dusting me off. The strongest, most stunning
woman I know. Who taught me that the word *love* is a verb
that involves putting others first. The person that has
infused in my heart to respect myself, even when others
neglect to see my value.

...You are loved beyond words.

WHO CAN BENEFIT FROM THIS BOOK?

The primary purpose of this book is to encourage people, middle school students to adults, through my personal pain, triumphs and stories. These stories have challenged and changed my life for the better. My hope is that you find value and healing within these pages.

-Tom Varano

FOREWORD

by Larry Broughton
Award-Winning CEO & entrepreneur, former US Army
Green Beret, No.1 best-selling author

Tom Varano invites us to travel with him on this captivating journey of self-discovery in "From the Pit to the Palace," demonstrating the importance of dreams, the strength of faith, and the transformational power of art while also reassuring us of our innate potential for greatness.

I'm blessed to have met Tom and some of his family at a patriotic event in Dallas, Texas where we were both presenting. I was there to deliver a keynote talk, asking the difficult question, "Is Integrity Dead in America?" Tom took the higher ground and delivered a powerful, spirit-moving performance. He stood on stage with several black canvas frames. Beautiful music played to set the mood while he painted stunning patriotic images that touched the hearts of the audience...but, it was his master storytelling in between his painting sessions about how life could be, and should be, that touched my soul.

Varano's book is a vivid canvas that has been painted with the colors of faith, resiliency, and hope. He effectively conveys the necessity to have faith in our own dreams because, no matter how private they may be, dreams depend on the faith of the one who is carrying them. They develop, materialize, and thrive in the supportive womb of belief. This idea recurs frequently throughout the book as he depicts his life through the prisms of success and adversity, passion, and purpose.

He skillfully takes us through the turning points that changed his course, demonstrating the strength in openness, the influence of choice, and the gatekeeper function each of us does in our own lives. His story serves as a reminder to pursue our passions with unreserved ardor because success, like a piece of art, demands a whole heart.

Varano's inspirational message of Dreaming B.I.G. serves as one of the fundamental teachings underlying his narrative. He skillfully explains how our route to success is determined by the books we read, the people we associate with, and the goals we establish.

The deep knowledge that everyone of us has a divine destiny is deeply woven into the fabric of his story. We can sense the resonance of his faith, the value of his trust, and the gravity of his appreciation in his words. This book serves as a reminder that our search to understand our purpose in life is what makes life so lovely. Once we do, our joy has no bounds.

He also underlines how success comes with responsibilities. Whom much is given, much is in fact expected of them. He exhorts us to live deliberately, to share our good fortune with the world, and to exert positive influence, a sentiment that is especially relevant in the turbulent times we currently live in.

Reading "From the Pit to the Palace" is like embarking on Tom Varano's own adventure. His observations and life lessons serve as a gentle reminder that we are all creators— not just on canvases, but in our own lives. We all possess the ability to produce works of art. Therefore, let this book serve as your road map, source of inspiration, and constant reminder that you, too, can climb out of your own pit and into your palace.

Explore these pages to discover your inner artist.

Larry Broughton is an award-winning entrepreneur and CEO, best-selling author, former US Army Green Beret, and an internationally-acclaimed keynote speaker. He makes regular appearances on radio and television networks to discuss personal development, entrepreneurship, strengths-based team building, and the leadership gap he sees growing across America. Visit Larry at www.LarryBroughton.me, and follow @larrybroughton on most social media platforms.

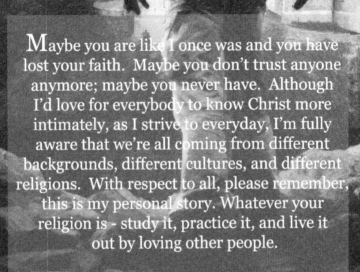

Maybe you are like I once was and you have
lost your faith. Maybe you don't trust anyone
anymore; maybe you never have. Although
I'd love for everybody to know Christ more
intimately, as I strive to everyday, I'm fully
aware that we're all coming from different
backgrounds, different cultures, and different
religions. With respect to all, please remember,
this is my personal story. Whatever your
religion is - study it, practice it, and live it
out by loving other people.

It's as simple as that.

TOM VARANO

INTRODUCTION

'FROM THE PIT TO THE PALACE'

STORIES OF OVERCOMING THE ODDS

Life is a tapestry woven with threads of joy, love, and laughter, but it is also punctuated by moments of immense pain and heartache. We all experience the bitter taste of adversity, loss, and trauma at some point in our lives. These painful events can shake us to our very core, leaving us feeling vulnerable, shattered, and unsure of how to move forward.

In the face of such challenges, it is all too easy to succumb to the weight of despair (which I reference as the 'Pit'), allowing the pain to define us and dictate our future. However, within the depths of our darkest moments lies an extraordinary power—the power of resilience, peace and hope (the Palace). "FROM THE PIT TO THE PALACE" is a profound exploration into the human spirit's incredible capacity to heal, grow, and thrive in the aftermath of the most painful experiences. In these pages, we delve into my personal stories of trials and heartache. By weathering the storms of our lives, and emerging on the other side, we have the opportunity to grow and become stronger and wiser.

This book serves as a guiding light for those who find themselves caught in the clutches of despair, reminding them that pain, though inevitable, does not have to be the end of their story. It unveils a roadmap, carefully crafted through personal narratives, psychological insights, and practical strategies, to help readers navigate their own journeys of healing and transformation. Drawing upon the wisdom and empathy from people who have cared, "FROM THE PIT TO THE PALACE" illuminates the pathways towards reclaiming joy, finding purpose, and rebuilding a life brimming with hope. It explores the intricate interplay of what it takes mentally and spiritually to rise above our pain and forge a new narrative for ourselves.

Within these pages, you will discover the resilience that resides within you, a resilience capable of turning suffering into strength, pain into growth, and darkness into light. You will learn to confront and process the haunting echoes of trauma, to harness the power of forgiveness and self-compassion, and to cultivate the courage to embrace vulnerability and rebuild shattered foundations.
This book is an invitation—an invitation to embark on a profound journey of self-discovery, healing, and transformation. It is a testament to the indomitable human

spirit and a beacon of hope for those who may feel lost in the shadows of their painful past. Together, let us embark on this journey, hand in hand, as we navigate out of the depths of pain and enter into our own 'Palace', stronger, wiser, and more resilient than ever before.

Tom

"WHEN WE ARE NO LONGER ABLE TO CHANGE A SITUATION, WE ARE CHALLENGED TO CHANGE OURSELVES."
-VIKTOR E. FRANKL

...KEEP CLIMBING

Chapter One

Living with Passion

Have you ever tried to read a book upside down? Try it!

Does it seem futile? Are the blurs and shapes difficult to make out, at best, and nonsensical at worst? Now, flip it right side up! The distorted lines become letters . . . the letters become words . . . and the words become sentences with powerful meanings. Just a simple flip. God sent His Son, Jesus Christ, to flip death into life. And He flipped my life from devastation into joy.

I'm Tom Varano. And this is my story.

"My name is Tom Varano . . . and this show is called Emotion Into Art. Thank you!" I remember the thunder of applause resounding throughout the theater, as I gave one final wave before walking off the stage. Within moments, the large black curtains slowly closed and my throat tightened with emotion. Using the back of my hand to wipe my burning eyes, filled with sweat and tears, I stepped into the welcomed darkness backstage.

This is it. It is what I have come to call the "Hand in Glove" moment. The moment when I realize, right now, as I stand in the dark shadows of this stage, *this is exactly where I should be.* It is the moment when I feel every fiber of my being stretched with both exhaustion and exhilaration, that I know, this is what I'm supposed to be doing. This is what God created me for.

It is a truth that only those who are courageous enough to live out their passions can fully understand.

Every show I give creates overwhelming emotions for me. I'm used to that. I love it. It means I've connected with my audience, and they've connected with my message as much as my art. That means everything to me. I remember that this particular show packed a stronger emotional punch that I wasn't prepared for. Maybe it was because it was the second half of a double-header show that day. The moment my final piece was presented, and the music began to fade throughout the electrically charged room, I was already overwhelmed with an intoxicating joy, like my own personal ecstasy. When the students all rose to their feet for a thunderous standing ovation, it nearly broke me - in the best of ways.

There, in that backstage darkness, a young student appeared.

"Mr. Varano," she started, just loud enough to hear above the applause.

Turning toward her, hiding my surprise at how she got backstage so quickly, I uttered, "Yes?"

I immediately noticed her tear-filled eyes and understood. It was not by mistake that I named my show "Emotion Into Art". It is not unusual for my audience to be emotionally moved on many levels. I am always humbled when it happens, but it comes with a responsibility. A responsibility that I do not take lightly. I cannot pour a message of following your dreams, living your passion, and going all-in with your life without being ready and able to rise to the occasion like this very moment – like this very moment, as this young student stood before me.

Typically, I have a few quiet moments backstage to recover from my performance before I face such encounters. A few moments to be grateful for what I do and to prepare myself for the interactions that follow. However, that was not the case on that day. I am acutely aware that how I handle these moments can have a profound impact on someone and it is something that I do not take lightly.

In this moment, this young student was hurting and confused. Gathering her courage, she took a shaky breath before timidly approaching me.

"You talked about living your dream," she said, her lips quivering with emotion as tears trickled down her face. "You talked about having passion toward your dream, but . . . " her voice breaking as my heart constricted with compassion, "what if my parents don't believe in my dream?"

And there it was - the cause of so much anguish.

This was not the first time I had been asked this question. It is a common theme that I recognize from speaking at middle schools, high schools, and college campuses across the country. I hear it in students' questions and comments after my shows; I feel it in their applause. I understand their need to voice these uncertainties.

These students are living an exciting time in their lives. The world is before them like a blank canvas. Some students are eager to be out from under their parents' rules, some are eager to escape difficult home lives. And many, like this young lady before me, are burdened with a fear about choosing between following a path to please their parents, or a path to pursue their own passions. These two paths do not always line up.

I'm a father. I understand that parents just want what's best for their children. I believe a lot of parents push their children into career paths the children have no interest in, not as a means of oppressing them, but out of a genuine belief that it is in the best interest of their children. Many parents simply advise based on their own limited views from their own childhoods, unable to bring open minds to the unique purposes for which God created their children. I believe most parents truly do want their children to live lives packed with purpose, passion, and security.

In that moment, I answered her with complete honesty. "Not everybody needs to believe in your dream," I told her. "Your dream first and foremost needs to be believed by you because you're the one that will be living it out." I assured her that her parents want what's best for her and that it's all right for her to choose a path her parents may not support. "They don't have to understand it, but you need to prove that you're willing to do the work, to carry out whatever it is you're passionate about." I then encouraged her to respectfully communicate her struggle with them. "It will be a difficult conversation," I counseled, "but it is a discussion that needs to happen. In the end, following your dream will depend on your hard work, determination, and vision."

This young woman had the chance to flip the expectations and path she would follow. And in doing so, her courage would allow a completely different outcome and happiness.

I was one of the lucky ones. Not long after high school I decided I wanted to become a portrait photographer. Although my father didn't understand my dream, he encouraged and supported me. I'm blessed to have had a dad who understood that the value of struggle outweighs the regret of never trying. He went so far as to allow me to transform two bedrooms in our home into a portrait studio and office. I will never forget the first summer I was in business – 200 high school students showed up at our house, knocking on our door and asking my dad where to go to be photographed.

This passion and hard work are the tenets I'm trying to convey to the students I perform for and speak to. Actually, conveying this message is my goal for every audience, no matter how old they are. Whatever you want to do, you should do it with your whole heart. That's what we need to focus our lives on. We need to find something that we love to do. Not something that somebody told us to do, but something that is in our hearts to do. You can't dabble with this thing we call a dream, because it is like sand in your hand - it will sift right through your fingers. It's fragile.

The conversation with the young student on that long ago day lasted no more than five minutes. I like to think she is out there today, living her dream with passion.

One of the most recurrent questions I receive from people is:

What do I do if I don't know what my dream is?

The best way for me to help them answer that question is to walk them through a process that breaks things down in such a way as to help reveal the passions they are carrying inside. Here is what I suggest.

First, make a list of the things you love and the things you enjoy doing. For instance, maybe you love animals and enjoy caring for them. Now that you've identified that, the next step is to ask harder questions. Why do you like taking care of animals? Does this caregiving bring you joy? Make a list of the pros and cons of what taking care of animals entails. Do the pros outweigh the cons? Next, you can begin researching various careers associated with working with animals. Study it out and choose which career you can see yourself pursuing. This may seem too simple of a process, but I think we tend to overcomplicate our decisions.

The path you choose can take you anywhere, but it will take you nowhere if you don't follow it.

I have a friend who loves animals, especially dogs. Yet, he didn't take the traditional route looking at career choices working with dogs. He thought outside the box. He started a franchise creating space as big a grocery store to care for dogs in an enjoyable atmosphere; a place for people who have busy lives, or who are going on vacation, or who want daycare and socialization for their dogs. The system he dreamed – became a reality as he embraced it and worked hard, and it is now an amazing place where people love sending their pets.

In the marketplace, we don't get paid by the hour, even though our paychecks may make it seem otherwise. In fact, we are paid by the value we bring to that hour. *What do you do to bring value to your own life?*

I'm proof that you can make money doing what you love. I'm an artist. I spent over 30 years taking portraits with a camera.

Now, I paint portraits on canvases for live audiences, where I weave the stories of the people I am painting into my performance. Each canvas, each story, carries a lesson.

I give all that I have for each portrait and performance. When I'm on stage I carry my audiences with me through storytelling. There are moments I'm silent allowing my words to sink in; other times, I jump down off the stage to join the audience. I encourage the audience to look at the person I'm painting. I talk about that person's life and what he or she did to overcome adversity and hardship.

I know the audiences grow to feel like they know the subjects – who they are and what they went through – by the end of the event, and I know that it gives them hope that they, too, can overcome the challenges at play in their own lives. They, too, can flip their realities.

When you see my performance, experience the emotions, and absorb the lessons, you may think this work is easy for me to do. But nothing worth having comes easy.

It's about showing up in your own life.

If there is something you want, you have to work hard to have it. You have to be afraid to want it, afraid to lose it, and afraid to try. If you feel that, then you know you are moving in the right direction to turn your passion into your purpose.

I'm here to tell you that artists can be successful. I'm here to tell you that ***you*** can be successful in building your dream just like I built mine. I will also tell you, in the pages of this book, about the struggles I overcame to get where I am today. My past is filled with challenges and trauma. Life is sometimes hard but I live with joy because I am living my passion. I am doing what I know God has called me to do with my life.

You can too. If you are experiencing the opposite of what you desire, you can flip your reality. It's never too late.

It's so important to have big dreams and to desire the things on the top shelf in life - those dreams and desires that appear insurmountable. At some moments they may be, but with time, education, hard work, and tenacity - you will be well on your way to achieving your top-shelf goals.

Now, imagine a stack of books being placed on a desk with topics ranging from health and spirituality, to finances, relationships, etc., and allow me to share my favorite acronym with you: B.I.G. You and I need to dream BIG! The "B" is for the books you read. I like to refer to this tall pile of books as a type of ladder. I live in America where we enjoy a ladder of success – how successful we are depends on how much climbing we do. I cannot emphasize enough the importance of reading - reading more than what is required by your teachers or professors. Read about what you love to do, experiment with new authors, or read about something new. What job do you want to have? Where do you want to live? What car would you like to drive? Learn how to create wealth for yourself or your family. Learn about interesting places to travel. And so much more! All of these questions and answers, and adventures are found in books!

The "I" is for the individuals you hang around. Think of the people you surround yourself with and then ask yourself, "Are these people pushing me toward my dreams? Or are they dragging me down?" If the people you surround yourself with are not supporting your dreams, you need to create a different group of people to spend your time with. People have the power to affect your life - both positively and negatively. Choose your circle of friends wisely.

Next is the "G". The "G" represents the goals you have on the path to achieve your dreams. What are your relationship goals? Your financial goals? Health goals? There are so many goals to aim for and to reach on the way to your dream that it's important to write them all down. Set yourself up for success by creating stepping stones that allow you to climb each rung of your ladder to success.

What value are you bringing to your own life?

The more value you pour into yourself, the greater impact you have on yourself and on others around you. In many cases the more value you are adding to meaningful areas of your life, the more they grow and become fruitful.

As high school students approach graduation there are a lot of emotions that arise: anxiety, fear, excitement, apprehension. It's important that when you choose your path, it's a path leading to where you want to go. Whether your path leads you to college, a trade school, an apprenticeship, or a job - it's important that it leads you to something you love so you can put your whole heart into it. If you find what you love, you will become a sponge and you will want to soak up as much knowledge as you possibly can. Sometimes college seems like the path of least resistance - a gateway between independence and the security of structured routines and parental oversight. Of course, college does play a critical role for many career paths and for many dreams to be built, but I encourage you to ask yourself the following questions before jumping into a path that does not do service to your passion or your dreams:

What do I want in life?

Am I going to college only for fun, or am I going because college is another rung on the ladder to my top-shelf goals?

Am I pursuing a degree in something I love or am I just eager to earn a high-dollar salary once I enter the workforce?

Let's talk about money. One of the rungs of your ladder may be to become wealthy. Money is important; it can buy you things; it has value to bring about the worldly items we may need to sustain us. Yes, money can create avenues for success, but it is not what life is about. Life is about enjoying experiences, learning new things, having meaningful relationships, and valuing things outside of the realm of wealth. Money isn't going to bring some of the important things into your life. Without passion and love for your life and what you do, there is no freedom. I will talk more about this in the following chapters.

There is a reason God breathed life into you. There is a purpose for your life. The journey of your life is trying to figure out what you are here for. That journey should not be something you dread. It should be an adventure. And it should stir excitement within you.

When you experience my performance, feel the emotions, and absorb the lessons I give, you may think doing this work comes easy for me. Flip that thought upside down and you have the truth. Nothing worth having comes easy. It is about showing up in your own life. Life is a study. In every area. If there is something you truly want, you have to work hard to have it. Bottom Line.

This message isn't just for students; it's important for people of all ages. So many adults continue to live a life they built without passion, living their life devoid of true joy. But it's never too late to flip your reality upside down.

At the end of the day - this is your life. What are you going to do with it?

Take the lessons I give you into your heart - live them - and you will be on your path to living a life filled with passion.

Key Takeaways from this Chapter:

1. Not everybody needs to believe in your dream. Your dream, first and foremost, needs to be believed by you because you are the one who's carrying it out.

2. Whatever you want to do, you must do it with your whole heart.

3. You can be successful in building your dream, just like I built mine.

4. Find out what you truly enjoy doing and set out to do it.

5. Dream B.I.G. - The Books you read, the Individuals you surround yourself with, and the Goals you set, will determine your success.

6. There is a reason God breathed life into you. There is a purpose for your life. The whole beautiful journey of your life is trying to figure out what you are here for, and when you do your joy will be immeasurable!

"FOR WE ARE GOD'S MASTERPIECE. HE HAS CREATED US ANEW IN CHRIST JESUS, SO WE CAN DO THE GOOD THINGS HE PLANNED FOR US LONG AGO."
-EPHESIANS 2:10

...KEEP CLIMBING

Chapter Two

Pit Living

We are all born into a story. A story filled with pages of moments in time that shape who we are; our own personal story where we can be both the protagonist and the antagonist, depending on what page we are reading.

I was born into my father's story.

Thomas Anthony Varano, an Italian-American, born on the fifth of May, 1932. He enjoyed a generally carefree and happy childhood before enlisting as a teenager in the United States Navy. Once trained to be a medic, he began his military career serving in the Korean War. It was an exciting and challenging time in his young life.

At the age most students are graduating from college, my father was being medically discharged from the military. In just a little under two years of service, he was carrying an injured soldier on a stretcher and broke his back, becoming a 20-year-old disabled war veteran, and flipping his situation upside down. The years that followed were difficult as he endured multiple painful surgeries and long hours of physical therapy.

The experience changed him.

By the time I was born, my father had been disabled for 18 years, he had been married three times, and was the father to six daughters. This man who had a contagious laugh with a charming, charismatic personality, was loved by so many. Yet, he was also a man who people respected, hated, and, most of all, feared. My father was not always on the right side of the law and rarely let anything get in his way when it came to providing for his family. He did whatever he felt necessary in order to get by.

My father had a great heart. He loved his family. But he just struggled. Drugs and alcohol were recurring themes in his story. His life had been hard, taking the joy that had once been such a big part of him and tangling it with a weariness that sometimes led to dark moods and violent outbursts. Even as a young boy, I understood this, and I learned to gauge the turmoil and to avoid it as much as I could, along with the rest of my siblings.

It didn't stop me from thinking that my father was bigger than life. I knew he wasn't like the other fathers that I encountered. He wasn't able to throw a football, play catch, or wrestle with me on the floor. As a child, I will admit, I felt cheated. But he did his best to make up for the lack of sports play by coming to every game I played in - and he didn't just cheer me on from the stands. My father brought a scorebook with him and recorded everything I did. I still have records of every baseball I pitched, every bat I swung, and every play I made in every game I ever played.

It's good times like this that I like to remember most about my father. These were the good days.

Unfortunately, at home, we never knew what would trigger his mood. Sometimes, we, as a family, would be laughing, having a fun moment together and it seemed like in the next we'd be ducking for cover. Obviously, there were moments in between the laughter and the anger - something that someone said or did that caused these irrational reactions - but as a child I didn't always understand the conversations around me enough to realize what caused the quick escalation of his temper. It wasn't until I was older that I realized that my stepmother knew how to instigate his tirades, and she enjoyed doing it. Once the yelling started, she would turn away with a smirk, her eyes gleaming with triumph. And in her triumph, we would all suffer. My father had the temper, but she knew how to manipulate it. The dysfunction in our household was equally formed by the two of them.

I remember specific moments happening quickly. In my child-like memory, an angry explosion would send us all scattering in fear, and then, as suddenly as it happened, it would be over, and my dad and I would be getting in the car to go fishing. Of course, we would have an amazing time – just a father and son, laughing and talking as if nothing terrible had happened only hours before. I didn't understand until I became an adult that as much as those moments fishing with my father were precious, I was also riddled with anxiety. As a child, I had an extremely difficult time processing the violent situations and at the same time worrying that I could possibly say or do something that would bring on another outburst.

And there are some memories that cannot be forgotten.

Memories like coming home from school to find my father in a panic, as he carried my unconscious stepmother across the lawn toward the house, hurrying inside, screaming at my sister and me to make the "concoction". The ingredients in the "concoction" were anything we could find that would help make her vomit. Together, as a family, we saved her from drug overdoses like this so often that it just felt like a typical day in our home.

Memories like the school bus coming to a stop in front of our house, and my stomach clenching with knots of fear and embarrassment as the remnants of a domestic dispute were on display in the front yard. Furniture, clothes, lamps . . . apparently anything they could lift and throw out the broken second story picture window would follow gravity to the ground below.

But, there are also many fun memories, such as the huge family gatherings we would have every week. My grandparents, aunts, uncles, nieces, nephews and cousins would fill our house most Sunday afternoons. There was always pasta, bread, and wine; every room would be filled with playful arguments and loud laughter.

Another happy memory I have is of my father and stepmother waking us up at three in the morning for a surprise trip to Disney World. On the plane, the pilots let us children come up and visit the cockpit. This was before the 9/11 attacks on American soil which prompted all the security restrictions we have today. I still remember the pure awe and joy I felt, sitting on the Captain's lap and staring out at the scenery through the flight deck windshield.

We had such a great time on this family trip. It was so normal.

This was the confusing and sometimes painfully chaotic pattern that was my home life.

I'm not sure why bad memories overshadow good ones.

I know that memories are generally prone to distortion over time and I'm sure some people would argue the finer details of these events, but the trauma they held was real to me. When I remember back, the memories are as clear to me as the day they happened.

It's hard for me to share these personal parts of my life - and I'm just getting started. It's difficult for me to talk about my father in a way that may sound disparaging. The truth is, in spite of the unintentional pain he caused us, we all adored him, and loved him beyond words. He truly was larger than life.

"Nine times out of ten, the story behind the misbehavior won't make you angry; it will break your heart." - A. Breaux

Given a brief glimpse of what my home life was like, I think it's safe to admit I was not an easy student to teach. My ADHD, the turmoil at home, and the typical youth issues of wanting to be anywhere but in school all played a role in this. Trying to focus and be a good student was extremely difficult for me.

I was a classic ADHD case. I would make careless mistakes and I couldn't remember the details of assignments or instructions. Paying attention was nearly impossible because I was easily distracted, and I would become easily overwhelmed and frustrated. It was almost painful to have to sit for any extended time and I was notorious for blurting out answers before my teachers could finish speaking. My teachers didn't know how to deal with me; they just wanted to survive me.

In those days we called Physical Education "Gym class", and Gym class was a special kind of nightmare for me. My Gym teacher was not equipped on how to handle a student like me. Not only did he make it obvious that he did not like me, he also verbally and physically abused me. He would embarrass me in front of the entire class, dragging me by my hair around the gym while he yelled, "This is what we don't do in class!"

In retrospect, understanding ADHD better, I can understand how challenging I was to instruct; yet, my behavior didn't warrant this kind of action disguised as discipline.

His treatment of me was confusing, humiliating, and hurtful.

He was wrong.

School should have been a refuge. Sadly, for me, it was not.

"MOST OF US LEARN IN CHILDHOOD TO "COPE"— WHICH IS TO SAY IGNORE, NUMB, MANAGE, OR REINTERPRET REALITY. WE DO IT TO SURVIVE, BUT OUR RELATIONAL INSTINCTS GET BENT IN THE PROCESS." - W. A. MORRIS

How did I cope?

I escaped.

Freedom was a feeling for me. A feeling I got flying through the air on my BMX bike. The faster I went, the better I felt. After school every day and on the weekends, I would ride the trails in the woods or hit the streets. I spent most of my time outside, riding my bike for pure enjoyment, with no plan of where I was going or who I would see.

On one of my escapades, I rode into the city and passed by a church festival. There were hundreds of people strolling through the church grounds, stopping every so often to have fun at a game booth or to stand in line to buy some "fair food".

And these carnival-goers were happy. I just wanted to be around them. No one seemed to mind the young boy cruising through the crowd on his bike, so I took my time and savored the delicious smells and the bright lights.

I was riding past one of the game booths when I stopped. Tiny fish bowls, each occupied by a single fish, lined the table. For a small fee, you could try your luck at lobbing a ping pong ball into a bowl. If your throw landed a ball in a fish bowl, you won a fish. I was mesmerized. I returned to this game every day of the festival. Eventually, the priest working the booth couldn't help but notice me. I had been expecting to be kicked out for loitering or annoying people with my bike, but instead he invited me behind the table to help work the booth. It was amazing to feel "seen", to feel like someone wanted me there with him.

This went on all weekend. I hated seeing the festival come to an end so I stuck around to help clean up, hoping to prolong this feeling of belonging. I had no idea how to make it last. As if he was aware of what I was thinking, the priest said, "You should consider attending church and becoming an altar boy."

My immediate reaction was apprehension. In my 12 years on this earth, I had learned that if something seemed too good to be true, it usually was.

The priest, whom I will call "Father T" was one of the younger priests in the parish - somewhere in his thirties. After spending the last several days with him, I felt comfortable. Besides, he was a father of the church; someone who was safe and trustworthy. So, I started regularly going to church services. I took classes and became an altar boy. I met other kids my age, who are, still, to this day, my good friends. It was everything I'd been afraid to hope it would be. I can't really describe how incredible it felt to be a part of something, to be accepted and valued in the Christian Youth Organization. The honor of being on the church altar, of serving God in that way - was an experience I'd never had before.

I was so grateful to the man who opened these doors for me. Father T had become more than a mentor in my life; he had become a father figure. A calm, peaceful even-tempered father figure.

It wasn't long into our relationship that he began taking me on day outings on his boat and overnight trips on the road. Then came the extravagant gifts. My family lived on a disability income and money was always tight. The popular toys and electronics were something my siblings and I could only dream of having, but Father T just gave them to me.

Needless to say, my relationship with Father T was not appreciated by my biological father. The closer I became with Father T, the more time I spent with him, the more gifts he bought me - the more my namesake father resented him. In time, my relationship with my own father became strained.

But at that time, at that age, it was worth it to me. I loved my father deeply, but the reprieve and validation I received from Father T had become a lifeline for me. So much so, that I ignored the small pit that appeared in my stomach the times I'd fall asleep in Father T's car, only to awaken and find my zipper down on my jeans. "Nothing bad happened," I reasoned with myself; "zippers don't always stay up. I probably forgot to zip it when I last went to the bathroom," were the thoughts I used to comfort myself.

A couple years into our relationship, everything fell apart.

The last weekend I spent with Father T started as usual - with excitement and anticipation. Father T shared a lake house with a group of families, and one weekend every summer, he was allowed to use the house and invite guests. This year, Father T invited me to join him. The massive, incredible house sits on a private island - just getting to it was an adventure in itself.

As evening came on our day of arrival, Father T and several children's parents gathered on the porch, while the teenagers gathered in the game room. Pool tables and games were available - it was a lot of fun.

We weren't in the room long before a friend of mine dropped down next to me on the sofa.

"Hey, Tom. What's been going on?"

It was an ordinary question and I responded in like.

"Not much."

"You spend a lot of time with Father T . . . how's that going?" he continued. "He do anything for you?"

With that question, the rest of the boys dialed into the conversation, inching forward until they formed a circle around me. I still didn't think that was unusual, so I shared some details of the trips Father T had taken me on, adding in details about the gifts he had given me.

"He's awesome." I told them.

My friend only nodded, knowingly. No one seemed impressed by the trips or the gifts. "Hey, do me a favor. We're going to all go back up to the house. When we go up there, all the parents will be on the porch. Just follow us into the house. Don't say anything, just follow us right in. Father T may ask you something but don't talk, just come in."

This was a weird request, but I agreed. So, up to the porch we went; we passed the parents and Father T. Just as my friend predicted, Father T called out to me. And, just as I agreed, I ignored him.

Well, the screen door had barely slammed shut behind me when Father T pulled it open and grabbed me by the arm, giving me a hard slap across my face. My brain was scrambling to process what was happening as this stranger posing as Father T pulled me into a room and closed the door behind us.

"Don't you ever, ever, ignore me when I call your name!" Father T screamed. I barely recognized the man. I was shocked and mortified, desperately trying to understand how this could be happening, when the other parents rushed in and pulled the raging priest away from me.

Helpless to stop the tears, I came completely undone in front of everyone present. The group of parents and teenagers rallied around me as they shared what part of me had suspected, but which I had refused to believe.

Father T was not safe.

Everything was exposed. Father T had been molesting not only me . . .but several of the other boys in that group.

"Tom," one of the fathers assured me, "We're going to get to the bottom of this."

It was a very long night for me.

The next morning, someone came and told me that Father T really needed to speak with me. This person asked me to take a short boat ride with Father T.

"We'll be right here," he told me, "Nothing's going to happen to you."

I was still in some level of shock and somewhat traumatized at the turn of events. I was devastated. The one person I believed I could trust, had broken my heart. So I went on the boat with Father T. He took us a short distance from the shore, turned the motor off, and began to apologize. I felt numb, but I listened.

"I'm sorry," he began, adding, "I have a sickness."

"I - I don't understand," I admitted.

"I need to get help because I molested kids and I don't want to hurt you."

He went on to explain that he was going to seek professional help and we wouldn't be able to see each other anymore.

I was confused and sad. I vaguely remember packing up and leaving the island.

By the end of the afternoon, I was dropped off at my house. I shared with my father what had happened and he was furious. He could only see red as he headed toward the front door, his intention to physically hurt Father T. I remember pulling on his arm, begging him to stay,

"Dad, Dad, it's over. He's sick. There's something wrong with him. He's going to get help."

I lost so much that weekend.

I lost my friend and mentor.

I lost what innocence I'd still maintained.

But most of all, I lost my faith.

I stopped going to church.

I stopped believing in good.

I stopped feeling seen.

I fell into a pit of depression.

It was a dark time in my young life. Years later, I would be led back to the church and to God, but until then, I wandered through life feeling alone and stuck. It felt like I was trapped in a vicious cycle of painful situation after painful situation where every time I thought I found an escape, it was just an illusion.

Have you ever felt like there is a dark cloud following you through life?

I certainly did.

During my time with Father T, I knew something was wrong, but said nothing. If I had spoken up, shared my thoughts with an adult, things would not have gone on as long as they had. If it hadn't been for the adults who intervened on my behalf, the abuse would have progressed. The other boys he molested were not so fortunate.

This abuse is happening right now.

Different place; different predator.

I know that some of you are living like I did - going home to a place with people you both love and fear. Or maybe there is no love, only fear.

If this is you, seek help. Be courageous and ask for help. If you do not have a friend or family member you can trust, approach your school counselor or school social worker. If they don't have the resources to help you, they will find you help.

Trust won't come easy, but you have to try.

You are not alone. You can flip your reality.

Four years later, tragedy struck again. This story is about my niece, Tania. As I mentioned earlier in the chapter, one of my fondest memories was how much time my extended family spent together. Due to my father's multiple marriages, my nieces and nephews were close to me in age. Growing up, I spent many weekends, summers, and vacations with all my cousins, nieces, and nephews.

As kids, we were all very close and we did everything together. Tania was truly beautiful, inside and out. She was the person who went out of her way to make everyone feel important; she was always kind. As teenagers, Tania and I were still close, but life was more complicated. Our immediate families were notorious for consistently falling in and out of favor with one another. One week, our families would spend time together, the next, we were enemies. Yet, Tania and I made a pact that we wouldn't let the family drama affect our relationship. We went to different high schools but we ran into each other occasionally at parties and we always instantly reconnected.

I never imagined a life without her in it.

Graduation weekend arrived, with numerous parties following. Although we both went out to celebrate, Tania and I didn't run into each other like we normally would have.

I vividly remember the day after graduation. It was beautiful and warm. The kind of summer day that you don't take for granted in upstate New York. It was the perfect day to mow the lawn. I never minded this chore because it always gave me time to think as I drove the mower around our property.

What I remember thinking about on that long ago afternoon, is blurred with pain.

I was thinking about the parties we attended the night before and how I was in love with my girlfriend, Karen. I know college weighed heavily in my thoughts. This moment in my life was packed with emotion as I prepared to step away from my intense childhood and into my college life to study computer science. But, I do remember feeling happy.

Until Karen came running out of my house.

My sister was on the phone, sobbing.

Tania.

Our beautiful, sweet and wonderful Tania had been killed in a car accident the night before.

This news sucked the air out of my lungs. Pain, like I had never felt, filled me. No, no, no . . . it couldn't be true, I remember thinking: "this is a mistake."

Last night Tania, her boyfriend, and another friend were leaving one graduation party to go to another. Their friend was driving and he was drunk, but Tania and her boyfriend got in the car anyway. He lost control of the car.

Tania was thrown from the car and was decapitated. She died instantly.

Her boyfriend was the only survivor.

Once again, drugs and alcohol had stolen irreplaceable treasures from our family.

My sister, Tania's mother, was broken. I don't believe she ever recovered from the loss of her first-born child. She fell into the pit, using whatever substance she could to numb the pain.

One decision and so many lives were destroyed.

"NO MAN IS BROKEN BECAUSE BAD THINGS HAPPEN TO HIM. HE'S BROKEN BECAUSE HE DOESN'T KEEP GOING AFTER THOSE THINGS HAPPEN." – C. Y. MILAN

So often my mind would scream, why do bad things keep happening to me? I used to feel like I just couldn't dig my way out of the pit of despair that seemed to follow me wherever I went. I began to look at myself as "that person". You know, the one that if something bad is going to happen - it's going to happen to me.

I was surrounded by friends and acquaintances who never experienced any kind of trauma, heartache, or tragedy. Why did they seem to dodge bad things and I couldn't? There were times I felt so powerless and miserable.

I felt alone.

Feeling alone is pit living.

Then something happened that flipped my entire reality. I found my way back to God.

The true power to change rested in my faith.

I noticed a significant difference in my life once I understood and was honest with myself that I was expecting bad things to keep happening. Yes, I experienced real trauma and bad things did happen to me, but I did not need to let these bad things define me. I finally became aware of how powerful my thoughts were and that the way I talked to myself, mattered.

I slowly started to profess, out loud, that good things were headed my way. I also started talking to myself with kindness.

And, yes, there were times I felt foolish doing it, but I didn't give up. Even on the days where my negative thoughts seemed to take control, I would force myself to follow up the negative with a positive. I didn't notice changes immediately, but in time, I felt the shift.

Expecting bad things to happen is a mindset.

Some call it the law of attraction. I had been allowing myself to be stuck in the pit, becoming a victim to the hardships of this life. I began to claw my way out, one handful of dirt at time.

Key Takeaways from this Chapter:

1. There's always help. There's always a way out.

2. Even when you want to isolate yourself, you have to take a chance and trust someone.

3. You are the gatekeeper of your life.

4. One decision can alter the course of your life, or even end it.

5. Expecting bad things to happen is a mindset.

6. There is a power in your thoughts and your words. Speak kindly to yourself.

My Dad and I

"DON'T WISH IT WAS EASIER, WISH YOU WERE BETTER. DON'T WISH FOR LESS PROBLEMS, WISH FOR MORE SKILLS. DON'T WISH FOR LESS CHALLENGE, WISH FOR MORE WISDOM."
-JIM ROHN

...KEEP CLIMBING

Chapter Three

Faith and Trust

Without faith and trust, it's very difficult to live this life. Without faith and trust, you are in that pit moment and you're withdrawing from everybody and everything, wanting to retreat from friendships, relationships, and family; not wanting to expose yourself to hurt and pain. Yet, without faith and trust in humanity, the world can be a very lonely place. It's not a good way to live.

That was my world for a long time.

A repetitive pattern was established in my life. I would start to lower my guard, start to trust, and even to hope for a better life - for better relationships. I would imagine myself crawling to the top of the pit, hanging on to weak roots with my arms straining as pebbles and dirt fly into my face. I would imagine reaching the top, my eyes just clearing the pit so that I could finally see a glimpse of the palace. A palace that was a haze of warmth in the distance, the magnificent doors slowly opening; a place filled with love, hope, trust, security, peace, and joy. Just as I would gather another handful of roots, I would slip and fall back into the pit. I could almost feel the vibrations of the palace doors slamming shut, the warmth suddenly replaced with iciness and total darkness.

The loss of my relationship with Father T was devastating.

Losing the relationship due to abuse made the loss more difficult to accept. But to be honest, it was the void left in my life where laughter, camaraderie, faith, and meaning had been that made it truly unbearable.

Because of what happened with Father T, I could not bring myself to go back to church. The hours and days I'd filled with serving as an altar boy, weekends filled with social events and Mass, now loomed before me, empty. The solace I'd found in prayer, the hope I'd found with faith, had been powerful enough to lift me out of depression and despair. Now that same power was flipped against me in what felt like immense cruelty.

The anger and loneliness demanded an outlet.

And I gave them one.

I was 16 years old, a junior in high school, and I'd made up my mind that I would never trust again. I started looking at the world with a deeply jaded lens. I now filtered every relationship, every introduction, through counter-productive questions:

What's the angle?

What do you want from me?

What are you trying to do?

How are you going to hurt me?

How are you going to let me down?

I tried to fill the void in my heart through other means. I dated a lot of different girls and numbed myself with drugs and alcohol. My father bought me a Firebird and I made that sports car my world. I filled some of the empty hours washing, polishing, and detailing that car. From the outside, it probably looked like I was having the time of my life. The truth was, no matter how many girls I dated, or how much marijuana I smoked, or how much alcohol I drank, my heart had a massive black hole and I was falling deeper down into it.

There is no way to fill a hole in your heart with emptiness.

Shallow, materialistic empty pursuits and possessions will never fill a heart. No amount of money or pleasure will heal a wounded soul.

It was a very dark time for me. I felt absolutely alone.

During this time, I was attending a Catholic school which was affiliated with Father T's former church, so the faculty was aware I was a victim of abuse. Although they were professionals and followed documented protocol by arranging for me to have counseling, this only added to my confusion. I was meeting with a priest at my school, to help cope with the trauma unleashed by another priest. It was difficult to make sense of it all. Of course, I felt absolutely no trust for my counselor and shared very little detail of what had happened with Father T. In turn, he didn't press me for details.

The years that followed were filled with highs and lows.

Long before the term FOMO was coined, I developed the habit of always looking ahead to the next "thing" I would do, hoping that this unsettled restlessness I felt would be alleviated. When the time came for me to go to college I thought - this is it! This was the moment I'd been waiting for - the moment I left all the disappointment behind and stepped into a career and life of my own.

Or so I thought.

Instead, I quickly realized I was taking courses toward a major that bored me to death. It felt more like a prison sentence than a new beginning. With the support of my father, I switched majors to one of my interests: Photography. I still wasn't going to church, but I'd finally found a positive outlet for my passion. One where I could escape into another world, disappearing behind the lens, and allowing me to frame the world the way I wanted to see it.

But, God wasn't done with me yet and neither was the Church.

One of the assignments from my college professor was to photograph the interior of a church. I hadn't been to a church in so long, I had no idea which one to go to. I know I'm dating myself here, but I flipped through a phone book, picked a church in my city, and called the listed number. Father Phillip A. Hearn is one of those people who smiles as naturally as most people simply breathe. Today, he's old enough to be called a senior citizen, but his soul is ageless. Always a joke on the tip of his tongue, his soft-spoken demeanor projects warmth and kindness.

"Absolutely," he replied, when I explained the reason for my call - even though I'd told him I wasn't a churchgoer myself. "Why don't you come down Wednesday night?"

He went on to say that the church would be empty so I would have privacy and as much time as I needed, promising to turn the lights on and even to play some music.

So, there I was the following Wednesday night - back in church.

It is a moment and an experience I will never forget, both for its breathtaking beauty and the profound change it brought to my life.

I was home.

All alone in the church, with the soft music playing in the background, I unconsciously ended the exile I had inflicted, and allowed the Lord back into my heart, one step, one photograph, one heartbeat at a time.

Click! I captured the painstaking beauty of each Station of the Cross.

Another click, and I captured the magnificent stained glass windows and the absolutely stunning paintings on the wall. By the time I reached the large crucifix, I was feeling confused and, oddly enough, emotional. There wasn't another person in the church as I stared up at the crucifix, but I didn't feel alone. As I stood there, without warning, tears came. I wept. In those quiet moments, I felt the Holy Spirit touch my soul and it broke me - in the best of ways. The experience broke down my walls and filled me with an overwhelming sense of peace and joy.

For the first time in a very long time, I prayed.

Later, at home, I sat in my overly indulgent suite my father had created for me. My suite was complete with its own bar, two bedrooms, a beautiful fish tank, an eight-foot pool table, and my own television. Normally, this was my sanctuary, but not this night. I was filled with an urgency that I had never felt before. I desperately needed to quench my parched soul; I needed to know more about this Jesus who hung on the cross.

I borrowed the 1965 American epic film, "The Greatest Story Ever Told", from my father. This film is the retelling of the Biblical account of Jesus of Nazareth, chronicling His life from the Nativity to the Ascension. Through the three-plus hour stretch, I experienced the life of Christ, and I wept . . . like a baby.

My whole life from that moment on was changed. It was unbelievable. I felt like it was completely flipped upside down. Everything was different.

It was intense and personal, and it is very difficult to try to put into words what exactly happened that night. It happens still, for me and to me, in different ways. It's this feeling of Grace I channel every time I am on stage, speaking my story and offering God's lessons, to my audiences.

I called Father Hearn back.

"I had an experience in the church and I just need to tell you about this because this is, this was, a crazy moment." The words poured out of my mouth from a place deep within me, and they had a life of their own.

Father Hearn listened to everything I had to say without interrupting me. When I was finally done, he smiled through the phone, saying, "I want you to come back. I want to speak to you."

I rushed to the church the very next day. There was no way I would have ever guessed what Father Hearn - or God - had in mind for me.

"I want you to be a sixth grade religion teacher," Father proclaimed moments after I sat down across from him. His words hit my brain but took some time before I could process them.

"What?" My confusion was evident in my voice and my expression. As fast as I had rushed to speak with Father Hearn the night before, I immediately felt myself wanting to retreat just as quickly. Was he crazy? Did he not hear me when I told him I don't even go to church?

With the gifts of hindsight and perspective, this memory makes me smile, because this is such a great example of how God works through others and in ways we could never conceive of for ourselves.

But I wasn't smiling then. I was panicking.

"I don't, I don't . . . think I'm ready for that. I just wanted to tell you that I had this experience." I couldn't stammer the words out fast enough.

Father Hearn was undeterred. He was also unshaken by my attempt to avoid the calling he knew was being placed upon me in that moment. "I understand, but I want you to be our sixth grade religion teacher."

He was wholly unconcerned with my lack of credentials, or the fact that I was only 18 years old, or my insistence that I didn't have enough knowledge to teach. In fact, he was laughing.

"No, no," he chuckled, with the soft laugh I would come to know and that I still love to this day. "I don't want you to think about it too much. I just want you to do it."

And that's how my spiritual drought officially concluded. I was suddenly a sixth grade religion teacher with a small class of students, forced to dive into scriptures and study so I could teach. I've always been an outside-the-box kind of person (thank you, ADHD). That is just who I am and how I think. And I don't turn that off. So, my class got to experience life with Tom "Outside-the-Box Varano" as their teacher.

We had a blast!

One evening, I took my class up into the darkened, quiet church. Turning the lights on, I gave each student a turn reading scriptures from the pulpit, right up on the altar, where priests and lay people usually stood. It was a coveted position. The effect of putting these students physically into that space was dramatic. Years later, I would occasionally run into one of these students, all grown up. As they talked about those moments in the life-changing time we had together in that class, it set a direction for my life. I realized that God wants to use my life in a positive way, and He hasn't stopped using it since.

Father Hearn and I are still friends today. I will always be grateful to him for literally opening up the door of trust for me. That is something that did not come easy for me. To a degree, it still doesn't. For me personally, it was coming back into the Church that really helped change that. The day I entered the church for an assignment, changed everything about my life. I immediately stopped using drugs. I reconnected with faith and trust. My wife, Karen, was my girlfriend at that time, and she, too, helped me to do that.

Do I believe my path walking with Christ is a journey in Truth and in Love? Absolutely. I feel it's my job to walk as closely as I can, identifying who Jesus is and trying to live as closely as I can in that Love, with Him as my guide. It's a lifelong journey because, we're human and we make mistakes. We mess up. We are weak sometimes in our thoughts and actions.

We are all fallible.

So, we have miserable teachers, pedophiles infiltrated in the Boy Scouts, sports organizations, and schools. These institutions in themselves are not corrupt but they can become disgraced by negligent leaders. There are diabolical people in all positions of society, sprinkled throughout all of our lives. The Church is not immune to the atrocious acts humans can inflict upon one another.

However, it would be a mistake to allow the sin of some to turn us all away from these institutions. Finding my way back into Church helped me heal in ways I never thought possible. I know not everyone will give church a chance.

But I hope you do.

My life has taught me that God truly loves us and ultimately He wants the best for us, even though our current situations may appear to tell us something different. It's because of knowing God and having a relationship with Him, knowing what He's done and continues to do in my own life, that I want you to have your own personal encounter with Him. And that doesn't mean it will happen as it did for me. God meets us individually where we are.

God's fingerprints are all over my life. Whether my life is good or bad, there is always a message He is trying to give me. He is trying to have me learn from my experiences, the good and the bad. If we can approach life this way, knowing that God has a message for us in everything, it will change our entire outlook on life.

So, when times are hard and you are hurting, scared, sad, confused, or angry, take a moment to look at your situation from the perspective that there is a lesson from God in all of it. And that lesson can unlock new levels of peace, happiness, and fulfillment for you and your life. That security, that fulfillment is palace living.

So many people spend their lives trapped behind doors God wants to unlock for them.

During these difficult moments, ask yourself these questions out loud:

What's the lesson here?

What would God have me do in this moment?

What is God trying to teach me?

Replacing the internal conversations I previously had when I assumed everyone was out to hurt and betray me and that I would never believe in anyone ever again, with these questions I asked God about the lessons being offered to me, is one of the most pivotal steps I have ever taken to create a life of happiness, hope, and love for myself and my family.

Did you know faith is a muscle?

Have you ever thought of it that way? Faith - believing in something even when you don't see it - requires repetition and exercise just like building any other muscle. The more you work it, the stronger it becomes. That's exactly how our faith works. *But Tom, if that's true, why are there so many examples of people who have faith and still suffer? If what you're saying is true, why do faithful people still suffer their whole lives, and why are some faithful people persecuted or killed?*

When we celebrate Christ's triumph over death, we remember, too, his passion and death - that He joined with the human race in the experience of fear, suffering, and sorrow. When we recognize God's presence with us in our despair, we are joining our sorrow with His and in that simple surrender, we join Jesus in his suffering. There is no love without suffering, and there is no suffering without love. The question we need to ask ourselves is will we accept both?

Whatever pain, whatever sorrow, whatever loss we endure, will be redeemed in heaven.

Now, I know for some of you, all this talk about God may be too much. Maybe you are like I once was and you have lost your faith. Maybe you don't trust anyone anymore; maybe you never have. Although I'd love for everybody to know Christ more intimately, as I strive to everyday, I'm fully aware that we're all coming from different backgrounds, different cultures, and different religions. With respect to all, please remember, this is my personal story.

Whatever your religion is - study it, practice it, and live it out by loving other people.

It's as simple as that.

Key Takeaways from this Chapter:

1. There is no way to fill a hole in your heart with materialistic items. There's always an emptiness to material things and shallow pleasures. You can't get enough money. You must fill your heart with meaningful pursuits. In my opinion, this starts with God.

2. God wants to use your life in a positive way.

3. Faith and trust are critical in life.

4. When times are hard and you are hurting, scared, sad, confused, or angry – take a moment to look at the situation from the perspective that there is a lesson from God in it. This really does help.

†

2 Corinthians 4:7-17 "But we have this treasure in clay jars, so that it may be made clear that this extraordinary power belongs to God and does not come from us. We are afflicted in every way, but not crushed; perplexed, but not driven to despair; persecuted, but not forsaken; struck down, but not destroyed always carrying in the body the death of Jesus, so that the life of Jesus may also be made visible in our bodies. For while we live, we are always being given up to death for Jesus' sake, so that the life of Jesus may be made visible in our mortal flesh. So death is at work in us, but life in you. But just as we have the same spirit of faith that is in accordance with scripture – 'I believed, and so I spoke' – we also believe, and so we speak, because we know that the one who raised the Lord Jesus will raise us also with Jesus, and will bring us with you into his presence. Yes, everything is for your sake, so that grace, as it extends to more and more people, may increase thanksgiving, to the glory of God. So we do not lose heart. Even though our outer nature is wasting away, our inner nature is being renewed day by day. For this slight momentary affliction is preparing us for an eternal weight of glory beyond all measure, because we look not at what can be seen but at what cannot be seen; for what can be seen is temporary, but what cannot be seen is eternal."

✝

Matthew 5:15-16 "No one after lighting a lamp puts it under the bushel basket, but on the lampstand and it gives light to all in the house. In the same way, let your light shine before others, so that they may see your good works and give glory to your Father in heaven."

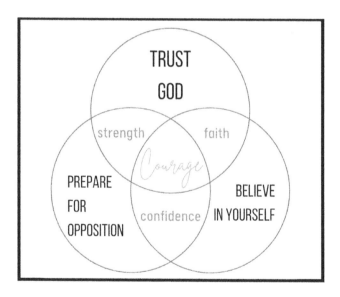

Used with permission of Coren Millikan at http:/CathingCourage.blog

"I LEARNED THAT COURAGE WAS NOT THE ABSENCE OF FEAR, BUT THE TRIUMPH OVER IT. THE BRAVE MAN IS NOT HE WHO DOES NOT FEEL AFRAID, BUT HE WHO CONQUERS THAT FEAR."
-NELSON MANDELA

...KEEP CLIMBING

Chapter Four

Lee's Lessons

I loved photographing people's weddings. With passion, hard work, and perseverance, I became very good at my job. Yet, even the greatest photographer can fail at photographing people, if he or she does not understand how to connect with them. Thankfully, I love people. I find everyone interesting. So, in my career, I not only use my talent, but also my energy to make people feel really good when I am in the room with them.

I brought this energy to every wedding I photographed. With my enthusiasm, I would make people smile just because I had a smile on my face. "Get together, get together!" I'd laugh and call out to them and they'd laugh, and then get together while I snapped a photo.

Along with my vibrancy, I brought my best wardrobe. I knew how to dress the part. I always wore tuxedos to my weddings. Even at my very first wedding shoot, when I barely had money to pay bills, I carved out funds for a tuxedo. No one there would ever have guessed that the happy, smiling, tuxedo-clad photographer could not feed his family without help from his parents. Or that his wife was working two jobs to help pay the bills, or that he had "no business" being in business for himself.

That's because none of those things ever crossed my mind; in my mind, I was living my dream. I had a beautiful wife I adored, and we believed so strongly in our path - we never felt like we were sacrificing anything. Rather, we felt blessed to be able to struggle together; to win and lose together.

We had almost nothing to our names, but we also had ... everything.

Sometimes, there are remarkable moments that change your life. For me, one of these moments happened early in my career.

I was at the reception of a wedding I was hired to photograph. Doing what I did best - interacting with the guests, having fun, laughing, enjoying myself as much as the guests were, all while keeping the checklist of the next important moments that needed to be captured.

"Young man, is this your business?" a gentleman asked, tapping me on the shoulder. I turned around as he continued, "I see you running around here with your camera - you're having a great time, aren't you?"

He went on to introduce himself. Lee Idleman was his name. All six feet something of him sat with some heft upon his tall frame; his thinning gray hair, eyes reflecting years of wisdom, covered by brown eyeglasses, all with a warm and welcoming smile, made me instantly comfortable. He had an amazing presence, possessing a natural, but rare ability to put people at complete ease while in his presence. We began to have "normal" small talk,

"How perfect the wedding had been . . . ."

"How the Central New York weather showed some mercy by giving the bride and groom a beautiful day . . . ."

"How long have I been in business? . . . ."

As we talked, Lee's wife, Sue, walked over to us as Lee commented that it was easy to see I love what I do, and to notice how people respond to me.

Apologizing for the interruption, she flashed a smile, asking "What's going on here?" My guess is that Sue was well accustomed to her husband's passion for changing people's lives and immediately recognized what was happening long before I would understand it, myself. Everything about Sue radiated class; from her clothes, to her hair, to her makeup, to her demeanor. She was a woman who paid attention to detail and, although significantly shorter than her husband, she projected her own friendliness to complement his perfectly.

Lee introduced his wife and then wrapped up the conversation with an invitation. "Look, Tom," he said. "I see something in you. I don't know what it is yet, but I don't normally see it. Do you have a business card?"

"I want to invest in you," he informed me.

And then we went our separate ways. He went back to his table and I went back to work.

By the end of the night, knowing I had successfully captured a memorable wedding for the bride and groom, my thoughts eventually worked their way back to my interesting encounter with Lee. There were so many questions running through my mind. Unfortunately, he and his wife had already left, so I carried those questions home with me. And within a day, I had dismantled the conversation as something that happens in a moment, but never really transpires into anything.

The following Monday, my phone rang and Lee's voice boomed from the other end, "Tom, do you remember me from the wedding?"

I smiled, "Of course I do." I was pleasantly surprised that

he followed through with the call, yet, also, a little apprehensive. "I actually wanted to ask you a couple of questions."

He invited me to ask away and I blurted out my confusion.

"Lee, you said you wanted to invest in me. Do you want to own part of my business? I don't understand." It was the biggest question I had about our conversation. My life experiences to date had taught me that no one offered anything without an expectation of something in return. I also had learned at an early age, if someone seemed too good to be true, they probably were not very good at all.

"No, no," he laughed, taking this opportunity to give me a little background on himself and what he did for a living. He explained that he worked for a company called Neuberger & Berman and managed $29 billion in assets for his clients in New York City. Money was the last thing he needed, he assured me.

Now he really had my attention. I was stunned into silence as Lee patiently waited for me to recover. Still convinced there was some hidden angle, I asked Lee what he wanted. His answer only confused me more.

"I want to own a piece of your passion," he said.

The business side of Lee kicked in then, and he moved straight to the point. "Look, Tom, I don't see myself in the upstate

Syracuse area anytime soon. Why don't you come down to Manhattan and I'll explain everything to you then."

I hesitated as Lee's words triggered my past, and suspicion and fear overwhelmed me. I was in full fight or flight mode, leaning toward flight. My overactive imagination was working hard as I envisioned all sorts of vile scenarios from the deadly to the perverted. I needed some advice and the first person that came to my mind was my father - my best friend, my rock. "Lee," I choked out, "Do you mind if I talk to my Dad and then call you back?"

Lee was fine with that, but added more mystery to the moment before we hung up. "Before you come down, I have an obligation for you. And I'll tell you what that is when you call me back."

I had barely hung up before I was out the door, driving to my father's house. I burst into the solitude of my father's home, where he lived alone, and babbled a mile a minute.

"Dad! You're never going to believe this!" I couldn't get the words out fast enough as I related the story to my father and ended with, "and now . . . I don't know what to do!"

My dad was an old-time Italian, screamer-guy. His response was immediate and delivered in full-blown Dad-style, with the flailing hands and the no-nonsense tone. "Go see the guy!" he bellowed. "He's not the don (his reference to the mafia)! Where's your faith? You're in church twice a week! Go see what he has to say! He's not going to hurt you!"

Whenever you have a loved one or friend behind a decision that you really want to make, there's more passion, more vigor. Having my dad support me in this leap of faith made it even more exciting for me. I couldn't wait to call Lee back.

I guess I could have called him from my father's house, but instead I drove back to my studio to make the call. "Lee, I have great news! My Dad said I could come and see you!"

Lee's amusement was evident, as was his appreciation for the way I was being totally transparent with him. Then he shared with me the obligation he'd eluded to earlier; I was to write down everything about my life - my marriage, my business, my dreams, my bills and my debts - he wanted to know everything there was to know about me. I agreed, as another thought occurred to me. I lived a couple hundred miles from the city and had never ventured to the Big Apple before. Would it be okay, I asked, to bring a friend? Now, this was long before the internet was available for the public. Lee consented and had two roundtrip airline tickets overnighted to me.

The night before our flight, I sat at my desk, thinking about one of the questions Lee had asked me about – my dreams. He wanted me to write a "dream" list of what I would like to see unfold in my life for the next six months to a year. I had never done that before. I knew what I loved to do, I knew about how to act on my passion, but I had never taken the time to put my dreams and goals in writing.

The next day we got in the car, and a few hours later, we were in La Guardia Airport, not far from Manhattan. It was the adventure of a lifetime for us. From the cab-ride, to the feel of the city streets, to the throngs of people everywhere. There was so much to take in, I couldn't decide whether to look straight up at the massive buildings or pay attention to navigating the people and the traffic. My ADHD was in overdrive.

Soon we were in midtown Manhattan, 605 Third Avenue, the offices of Neuberger & Berman. The glass building soared into the sky. Lee's office was on the 40th floor. When the elevator doors opened. Lee was standing right there waiting for us. My whole body shook at his handshake. "Boys, follow me," he said as he led us to his jaw-dropping corner office. It was like nothing I'd ever seen before, with its floor to ceiling glass. I was definitely in another world.

I put my stuff down on his desk and went right to the windows. The people below were so small. As I stared out in awe, I saw the Empire State Building and the Twin Towers! I was mesmerized, but there was business to be taken care of and Lee was ready to discuss why he sent for me.

My friend and I took our seats. Lee leaned over from the other side of his enormous desk to point at me. "Tom, tell me about your life."

I proceeded to tell him about my new marriage, my business, everything, just like he'd asked me to. Suddenly he cut me off. He'd heard enough. Rising to his feet, he pointed at me again and announced, "I have to invest in you. Something's telling me in my heart, I have to invest in you."

I still didn't understand what he meant, but I was there and in faith, I was fully committed to letting this experience play out. Lee then asked me if I brought the information he the information on my life, my bills and my debts - all my finances. I handed him the envelope I had prepared. My friend and I sat in silence as Lee splayed my entire life across his desk, not saying a word. Everything was written out about my life, as he asked. The silence carried on even when he pulled a checkbook from a drawer. We watched in amazement as Lee methodically wrote checks to pay every single bill and debt in that folder. Lee wrote and wrote until $65,000 worth of debts was taken care of.

My nerves were a jumbled mess for the eternity it felt like, sitting there watching Lee write check after check. It was like I was watching a movie of someone else's life. Finally, I lost the struggle to remain still and silent. Some part of me could not accept that this was happening. Some self-destructive part of me didn't believe I deserved it. I went to his side of the desk and grabbed him by the wrist as he was writing. "Lee," I said, "I really appreciate this but I can't pay this back."

"This isn't about you paying this back. This is about you helping somebody in the future and has nothing to do with you paying this back," he replied. Still not sure he understood what I was saying, I explained that I was a photographer and I didn't make that kind of money. Unfazed, Lee repeated this had nothing to do with money, and everything to do with me doing good for somebody else in the future. Then he wrote me a check for $22,000 and told me to, "Get that business off the ground."

I returned from New York City with a new life in my grasp. I couldn't wait to tell Karen! It was amazing. Just unbelievable, really. It was just a few weeks prior that I'd dropped my Italian gold-nugget ring in the church offering basket because it was all I had to give, and now our prayers had been answered.

We were able to implement changes in our life almost immediately. Karen was able to quit her second job. We were able to move the studio across the street from our "cozy" apartment into a commercial building on the corner, with a storefront. We renovated the space and transformed it into a working studio.

Understandably, it was an emotional time for us.

For the next four years of my life, Lee flew me to New York City every single month just to have lunch with me. It took me all day to travel there and back. I now have a love/hate relationship with LaGuardia, JFK, and Newark airports. I got stranded in those airports more times than I could tell you. But, it was worth it.

The hour lunch would go something like this:

I'd arrive at his office.

His secretary would let me in.

We'd shake hands and go to the windows.

We would check the weather in the city by the Twin Towers. If it was a cloudy day, you could just see the tips of the Towers popping out through the top, but if it was a beautiful day, you could see for miles down the Hudson.

We'd make our way to the elevator and head to a ground level cafe.

As soon as we got in the elevator, the doors would close and the lessons started for my life.

The elevator would be full of business people who would want Lee's attention, but he softly put them aside, **because he was with me**.

That's one of the most significant lessons Lee taught me through his example - wherever he was, he was present in that moment. He wasn't distracted. Whomever he spoke with had his full attention. Now, you and I - we're so inundated with technology, we have become so dependent on our cell phones - that we're not always fully present in the moment we are in. When somebody is saying, "Hey, can you please put the phone down?" what they're really saying is, "I'm here. And I want to be with you right now. I care about you and I want to interact with you." But we get so engulfed in our virtual worlds that we're missing heartbeats of our loved ones.

We were all born with a certain number of heartbeats that are going to come and go.

And that number is constantly clicking down. It's important for us to consider what and where we're spending our time. If we're not purposeful with our time or we're giving the wrong people our time, we are wasting those precious heartbeats.

Our time is precious. When I'm on stage, speaking to my audience, I'm very aware that their time is also precious. I don't take their time or mine, lightly. It's so important to ensure when we're in somebody's presence we're giving them our full attention.

One of the biggest lessons on being purposeful with our time presents itself when we have lost someone close to us. When you lose a loved one, you can't help but regret your lost time. I would do anything right now to have a cup of coffee with my father; to talk about his day, to listen to stories of his childhood. Unfortunately, I can no longer do that. I lost my father many years ago. How many of his heartbeats did I miss because I was too involved with my own life?

We're trying to wind up this life, let it go, and see what happens. And it's not going to work out. That's not how this works. It's intentional. We need intentional living. You and I both need that. We need to encourage each other in that, to be intentional with our thoughts, to be intentional with our character, to be intentional with our virtues. It doesn't just happen.

Once we reached ground level, Lee and I would make our way out into the streets. Every time I met with Lee he would tell me, "I want you to go and do this for somebody else. It doesn't need to be much." From the first time I went to meet Lee, his words replayed over and over in my mind.

How do you do this?

How do you help people without using large sums of money like he did?

Before I met Lee, I was the guy who went to my studio with blinders on, focused on my craft. My life changed in a thousand different ways after I met Lee. Finances had only been one of those changes. I started to pay attention to life around me. I began to look at people and their situations differently.

Over the next few years, my wife and I bought a home and started a family, as we continued to build our business. One morning, I was just about to enter my studio and I will admit, I had seen kids playing on the street many times, but this day, I actually found myself focusing my attention on them. On one in particular. A young boy in the back of my property was hammering nails into my beautiful oak tree. Stepping out back, I called out to him.

"Hey, man," I said, "come on over here. How old are you?" I asked the young boy his name and he told me. Then told me he was eight years old. "Aaron, what are you doing on the streets? It's dangerous out here." At the time I really had no idea where I was going with this conversation. I was just letting it unfold to see where it would lead.

"We're bored," Aaron said. "There's nothing to do." This, I could do something about. Telling Aaron to sit tight, I went into my studio down in the basement and retrieved a rake. "See all these leaves around the studio?" I explained. "How about you rake these up?" I reached into my pocket and pulled some cash out, showing him. His eyes got big. "If you clean up the yard, I'll pay you," I told him. He eagerly agreed and got to work.

Sixty minutes later there was a timid knock on my door. "Mr. Varano, I raked up all the leaves. Can you come and check it?"

Inspecting the lawn, there was not one leaf left. "Aaron, you did a fantastic job, man!" It felt amazing to see his face light up with my words and I handed him his hard-earned money. I was doing exactly what Lee wanted me to do and I vowed to keep my eyes open for my next opportunity to do so again.

To my surprise that opportunity came knocking for me the

next day - literally.

Tap tap tap . . . I heard on my door. I opened the door and it was little Aaron. He was asking me if there was anything he could do for me today. And that was the start of it. Aaron came around most days, continuing to do odd jobs for years. When he was about 14 years old I started bringing him to our home. He'd drive our mower around the yard with the happiest grin on his face. It almost looked like he should have a cigar hanging out of his mouth, that's how confident and cool he looked. I was in our swimming pool spending time with our daughters. They were thrilled, Dad is home! And there was Aaron cruising around the yard on the mower.

Eventually Aaron faded out of our lives.

I don't remember exactly how or why. Time moved on and his life moved in a different direction. I thought of him often and wondered what had become of the first person I had invested in like Lee had done for me.

Our lives moved forward, too, and our daughters were now in high school. One day Karen and I got the call every parent hopes to never get. Our daughter was crying and screaming into the phone, telling us she'd been in an accident and to come quickly. It felt like it took all my strength to stay calm, to talk my daughter down so she could give me the address where she was. Karen and I dropped everything and raced out the door, making our way as fast as we could to our baby. Blocks away, we heard the sirens. Rounding a turn the lights came into view, with emergency vehicles everywhere, blocking the road and time seemed to slow down. I remember everything about that afternoon in the greatest detail; the smell in the air, the sounds around me, the first responders.

I had never been more profoundly aware of what mattered most in my life as I was in that moment.

Flinging my car door open, I abandoned my wife and our vehicle in my full-on frenzy to reach our daughter. I ran faster than I'd ever run down those blocks until I pushed my way through the crowds and to my daughter's crumpled car. The impact had been great enough that the airbags had inflated. My daughter was still in the driver's seat crying as I pushed everyone away. I shoved until I was face to face with her, leaning into the car. "Jordynn, Dad's right here. I'm here, Jordynn!" I repeated over and over, as my daughter just kept crying. I was vaguely aware of someone's hands on my daughter's neck, protecting and stabilizing her while the crews worked to free her. Then a strangely familiar face peeked over the backseat as a young man said, "Mr. Varano, she's going to be okay."

Those trained, protective hands belonged to Aaron!

He had become an EMT! That was his dream and he had worked hard and achieved it! Aaron was the first one on the scene. He was driving the ambulance that day. There was this little boy who raked my leaves, now a grown man, rescuing our daughter. Instantly, my mind went to Lee's face. This is what he'd been trying to teach me. I finally understood. No amount of money on this entire planet could have bought the amazing grace I felt in that moment.

You and I have opportunities every day to pay our good fortune forward, to do good in this world.

To treat others with goodness and kindness. There's enough evil going on all around us. Let's just be a force of good. Let's do the right thing.

I was 23 years old when Lee opened the world up for me. Lee's gift was extraordinary, but it didn't mean I just sat back and lived off his generosity. Quite the opposite, in fact. I felt even more pressure to build and succeed, now that Lee had invested so much into my success. I was not going to let my family or Lee down. I worked harder than ever. I was on a mission for people to see themselves as beautiful. I developed my own signature style of photography. My clientele grew until I was booked for months in advance, with people traveling sometimes hundreds of miles to have me photograph them. I was no longer the photographer taking all the brides whose first, second, and third choices in photographers were booked. Now, I was the first choice.

Then there was another side to Lee's gift, and how it had springboarded our success on many levels. A ripple effect neither Karen nor I was prepared for. Some friends and close acquaintances began to withdraw from us. Sometimes someone would share an unkind comment with us about the money we were making, or a car we bought, or our home we moved into. The resentful comments hurt us to the point that we stopped sharing what was happening in our life. We hadn't forgotten what our life was like before our debts had been paid and we tried to be sensitive, but words weren't needed to breed jealousy and contempt. People would judge, based on appearances and even some of our friends who *did* know what was going on became resentful.

We helped many people by employing them - including many of our friends – but still there was resentment. There was also betrayal. We had never factored in the possibility that people would be jealous of our good fortune. We knew we continued to work hard and that our intentions were pure. We had the opportunity to keep everything Lee had given all to ourselves, but it wasn't our nature. What was given to us - we shared with our friends and loved ones. Paying off debts, trips, and dinners. If we saw a need, we tried to help. So, we didn't understand this negativity. The friends who did stay by our side were loyal and true; their strength of character, evident, which helped us guard our faith and trust in humanity.

One of the lessons Lee indirectly taught me was that relationships will change as you achieve your goals and build new success.

You will lose relationships. But you will also gain new ones, and you should never allow fear of losing a relationship be a reason for holding yourself back. I'm so grateful Karen and I stayed committed to our path and the calling I continue to feel. It has led us to so many new relationships and allowed me to impact lives in a way I never imagined possible.

When I speak about the pain attached to life's struggles, I am speaking from the heart and from experience. We all have the ability to change lives. It doesn't have to be all about us and what we can gain. We *can* help other people.

We may never know how many lives our actions impact.

Key Takeaways from this Chapter:

1. Be grateful.

2. It's so important to ensure that when we're in somebody's presence we're giving them our full attention.

3. We need to live intentionally.

4. You and I have opportunities every day to pay our good fortune forward, to do good in the world. There is enough evil going on. Let's just be a force of good. Let's do the right thing.

5. Relationships will change as you achieve your goals and build new success. You will lose relationships. But you will also gain new ones, and you should never allow the fear of losing a relationship be a reason for holding yourself back.

"THOSE WHO ARE HAPPIEST
ARE THOSE WHO DO THE MOST
FOR OTHERS."
-BOOKER T. WASHINGTON

...KEEP CLIMBING

CHAPTER FIVE

Giving

I know what it's like to feel as if you have nothing to give. Maybe everything you once had has been lost. Or maybe you've simply never had much in the first place. Maybe you've been pushed so far out on a ledge that you are using every drop of strength you have to hold on. And then someone comes along and tells you to let go of your worries and anxieties.

And you think they're crazy.

Surely if you let go - if you take just one hand off that ledge to try and pull yourself up higher, your other hand will not be strong enough to hold you. You will fall.

Right?

What if I told you the opposite is true?

What if I told you that it's only by giving everything you have that you will be blessed with abundance?

This doesn't have to mean financial abundance. Sometimes it's giving our hopes, our love, or our trust. Sometimes it's giving our time and service to others. Sometimes it's just showing up one more time.

I know what it's like to have literally zero dollars, to be dependent on others for help even though I was working as much as I could and trying so hard to be a good person, who does good things. I relate to moments when it feels like the only thing you can do is to hold on as tightly as you can, telling yourself you have nothing to offer anyone.

I also I know that sometimes, those are exactly the moments we are meant to let go. Sometimes those are exactly the moments we are meant to give the very shirt off our backs, if that is all we have to give. Letting go and giving away something you can't imagine being without is the *only* move.

Have you ever heard the saying "give and you shall receive"? This saying is actually based on a Biblical scripture. "Give, and it will be given to you. A good measure, pressed down, shaken together and running over, will be poured into your lap. For with the measure you use, it will be measured to you." (Luke 6:38)

I thought I understood this principle as a young adult and always believed myself to be a giver. My wife and I donated to our local homeless shelter every month. If I saw a homeless person walking on the streets, I would stop and bring them somewhere for a meal or take them food. If my wife and I were out to dinner, we would buy the family next to us their meal. If in a drive-thru, I would pay the bill for the person behind me. But was it enough? Up to this point in my life, I gave when I could and only when it was comfortable for me.

Little did I know the lesson I would be taught about giving, that I will never forget. It has continued to teach me throughout my life. It was uncomfortable and humbling.

Let me begin by telling you about a very special woman who made a difference in my life - my great Aunt Minnie. My Aunt Minnie and Uncle Joe never had children of their own. As a child, Aunt Minnie had been my advocate. While I certainly had enough trauma in my life, her kindness and attention seemed to take away some of that sting. When it came to me, Aunt Minnie was protective, generous, and caring.

Growing up, we never had much money. My father had to manage on such a limited income with a houseful of kids, that there never seemed to be enough. With that being said, it's not surprising that I didn't have much in the way of material possessions. The few things I did have were precious to me. So, the day Aunt Minnie surprised me for my birthday will forever be in my memory.

It was a weekend close to my 15th birthday and my Aunt and Uncle invited me to come to the mall with them. It wasn't an unusual trip because they enjoyed having lunch there and my aunt loved to window shop. As we passed a jewelry display case in the middle of the mall, one of the rings in that case caught my eye. It was a men's gold nugget ring. Now, you have to remember, this was in the 1980s and these rings were popular at that time. Well, I knew that I could never afford something like that, so after a brief yearning for the ring, I moved past and continued to browse. Aunt Minnie didn't miss much. She caught that moment, but said nothing. While I continued to look around, she called the jeweler to come over. I didn't pay much attention when something was removed from the case and she walked to the cashier. I thought she had found something nice for herself. But, oddly, she walked over to my Uncle and I wearing a big grin. When she reached us, she handed the bag to me. I was dumbfounded. It was an extraordinary thing to do. That ring became one of my most cherished possessions that I almost never took off.

Fast forward about eight years ahead and I was a 23-year-old newlywed. My wife, Karen, and I were working hard to pay rent on two apartments. Karen and I both believe the scriptures. We knew that if we worked hard and did not give up, God would provide opportunities for us to provide for ourselves. These were difficult times. I mean, who wants to work in a bank all day and then go clean hotel rooms until midnight, like Karen did? And although I enjoyed my work at the YMCA as an afterschool Site Director, it was hard holding that job down while building my business. It was hard, but we were in love. We were going after our dreams. And we knew in our hearts that God was going to provide. In the meantime, we gratefully accepted help from our parents, who, when needed, stocked our fridge with food for us. We accepted being limited financially as being part of the path to bigger things.

My path in life up until this point had been packed with a powerful blend of blessings and adversity. With the help of people like Aunt Minnie and a handful of others who supported me, I had somehow, surprisingly, landed in a life I was happy with. I had a wife I loved more than I ever imagined it would be possible to love someone. We didn't care if our apartment was small and our life was simple. I could have given up on my dream to build a photography studio. Instead, I just remember being so grateful that I never spent any time worrying about money. I was on a career path that filled me with excitement and which I knew would somehow lead me to success. Without knowing exactly *how*

I was going to build success for my family, I just knew that somehow I *would* - if I trusted in God and His plan for me, while working hard.

My reconnection to my faith was the greatest gift in my life then and the greatest gift still today.

That faith has allowed me to look upon my world as filled with blessings, where others may see only burdens. Think about it – would you rather live your life feeling joy and gratitude or fear and doubt? You need to realize, how you feel about yourself and your life, will overflow into how you live your life and how others respond to you. Wouldn't you rather trust that there is a plan for you? Trust that everything you are going through right now will make sense one day and through these hardships you will be stronger for it? Rather than feel like a victim in life? Living like a victim is *pit living* and it will keep you discouraged.

For me, faith and trust made all the difference.

About a year before Karen and I were married, we temporarily stepped away from the Catholic Church. After an invitation from a friend, we started attending a non-denominational church. We were not only attracted to the welcoming nature of the parishioners but the spirit and energy of the band music. We began to study the scriptures in a way that was new and exciting for us. We stayed at this church for 12 years before we eventually realized the Catholic Church had been, and always would be, our home.

During our time at the non-denominational church, we attended services twice a week - Wednesdays and Sundays. If you're familiar with church, you know about the collection basket that is passed around. This is the part in the service where churchgoers place a tithe or offering of some kind in the basket. This type of giving reflects a grateful heart that wants to give back to God a portion of what He has given us; in reality, it is already His. It's an opportunity to show God that He is first in our lives. This was something Karen and I took very seriously.

One Wednesday, Karen and I were in church. It had been a particularly hard couple of months. The strain of working four jobs between us and stretching our finances as much as we could, had us arguing over small, insignificant things. We hadn't lost faith, but we were weary. When it was time for the offering basket, I felt the heaviness in my heart. I had nothing to give. My bank account was depleted, my wallet empty. I remember praying, "Lord, I have nothing to give to you. I have nothing to give, but I *want* to give something." After my prayer, I slowly looked down at my hands and saw my ring. Quickly looking away,

I thought, no, not my ring, Lord. My Aunt Minnie had died years before that night and it was all I had left of her. Everyone who knew me *knew* how important my ring was to me. Pushing through the emotional pain, my eyes slowly came back to my ring. I didn't want to part with it but I knew what I had to do. I slipped that ring from my finger one last time. I rubbed it gently as I waited for the basket to reach me, my heart pounding in my chest. Without telling my wife, I tossed the ring into the basket. As hard as it was to let go of something so meaningful, the minute it hit the bottom of the basket, I felt not one ounce of regret.

All I felt was an amazing grace.

To this day, I've never given anything with the same level of innocence and gratefulness as I gave that ring to the Lord, on that day.

Four days later, in the early hours on Sunday morning, my rear car window was smashed, my stereo and Bible were stolen.

I'm not sure why these things happen. It was discouraging and it threatened to steal my joy, but no one was hurt. It could have been a lot worse. When Karen and I arrived at church we shared what happened with one of our best friends, Emmy Lilholt, and her face lit up with joy. "Do you know what this means?" she exclaimed, then laughed and gave me a hug. She then reminded us of a scripture that reads, "The thief comes to steal, kill and destroy, but God brings full restoration, to the point where our lives are overflowing. He makes everything better than before!" Hugging both of us this time, she offered, "I'm so excited for you both!"

Six days later I met Lee.

For the first time since my initial phone conversation with Lee, I realized that *this* is what God is talking about. *Give, and it will be given back to you.* I couldn't stop thinking about the ring I had given that night at church. In my heart, it was all I had of any worth to give and I obediently gave. My heart had been pure in my offering. Could the two events be intertwined? Could offering a gift with a pure heart and having property stolen from me have prompted this incredible gift of Lee?

I believe it did.

Little did I know, God wasn't done with my ring.

Fast forward another seven years. So many things had changed for me - my family, my business, my friendships, and people I had lost. My Pastor had been watching me grow in my life and in my faith. One night he asked me to stand in front of the church and tell my story.

So up I went. Standing before the congregation in that small church I told the story of meeting Lee and the impact this man had on my life. I included the part about what my life had been like back then and of placing my ring in the basket. I was concluding my talk, when suddenly my Pastor rose from his seat.

"Stop! Stop!" he called out. "I'll be right back!" He hurried from the room, leaving the rest of us waiting in bemused attention. When he returned just a moment later, he reached out to me while saying, "This is yours." It took me a moment for my brain to process what my eyes were seeing and my hand was feeling as the pastor placed my ring in my palm, explaining, "We found this in the church basket and we didn't know whose it was. We put it in the church safe."

At that moment, I realized that if we're doing things with the right heart, especially giving, we can never "out-give" God. I understood that God looks for the virtue within us to become the people He wants us to be. Have you seen this happen to someone? Someone who is committed to their path with an unwavering faith and who overcomes every obstacle they encounter. They exercise their faith muscle. And that's what I did with giving that ring.

When we give, we must do so out of gratitude.

We shouldn't give just to be seen giving. You'll never pull a fast one on God because He sees your heart and motive. He sees all. He knows why people are doing what they're doing. Sometimes no matter how pure our intent is or may have been, we find ourselves tainting the spirit of giving by seeking accolades for our good work. For instance, you have probably seen social media videos where someone approaches a homeless person and buys them a meal or gives them money. That person who is receiving the gift is surprised and grateful. Wouldn't it be more meaningful to simply slip that person a hot meal or some cash and not tell anyone what you've done? Shouldn't the feeling of knowing you've made an impact on someone's life be enough?

I think the biggest challenge is to avoid the need to be seen giving. Jesus performed miracles like helping paralyzed people walk and blind people see and He would tell those people not to tell anyone. Jesus said, "Watch out! Don't do your good deeds publicly, to be admired by others, for you will lose the reward from your Father in heaven. When you give to someone in need, don't do as the hypocrites do - blowing trumpets in the synagogues and streets to call attention to their acts of charity! I tell you the truth, they have received all the reward they will ever get. But when you give to someone in need, don't let your left hand know what your right hand is doing. Give your gifts in private, and your Father, who sees everything, will reward you openly." (Matthew 6:1-4)

Now this doesn't mean there is not a time and place to share your good work. Raising awareness for a good cause or volunteering our time are only some of the many worthy acts of giving.

Maybe you are reading this and thinking this isn't true because your faith is strong. And you give your time and resources but you never have anything amazing happen to you. Maybe you've heard of others who give everything they have to help others or do good work, only to suffer horrible fates.

Maybe you know someone who was like an angel in your life, who sacrificed so much for other people all the time without asking for anything in return, but they still got sick and died.

Maybe you are that person, continuing to fall short of your goals and dreams while helping others reach theirs, and wondering why God has not rewarded you.

I get it. It can make it all seem unfair and pointless. It can tempt you to stop giving so much of yourself, when all it leads you to is a life of struggle while the people you help leave you behind.

This is when we really discover who we are and what we really want our lives to be about. This is when we either grow or remain stagnant.

It's easy to give when we have an abundance. But who is to say what "abundance" really means? Some people have wealth, fame, and constant good fortune while you experience what feels like constant struggle. But that does not mean they are given abundance and you are not. It does not mean they do not have struggles you do not see. What other people experience and do with their own lives is *their* path. You have an opportunity to be a part of other people's paths. What you make of that opportunity is your choice.

I can tell you this: You *are* being given abundance right now. Today. In this moment and in every moment. You may just be struggling to recognize that abundance.

I struggled when I was a child. I didn't feel like I had anything to give because I was always experiencing one challenge after another. I didn't realize that even while people like Aunt Minnie were giving so much to me, I was giving right back to her. She was receiving my love and she was enjoying being a part of my life. For everything she had that I did not, she did not have a son to love her. Me, being there to fill a piece of that void in her life was a gift to her as much as her presence in my life was a gift to me.

Sometimes it is as simple as that.

Sometimes our mere presence is the gift we have to offer.

A conversation, a smile, a helping hand, a hug, or any one of the endless small ways we can show up for one another. We all have the ability to give that. And we all receive those things from others, even if we don't recognize the gifts. By being alive we are being gifted with an abundance of heartbeats. No matter how much we achieve in life we will always face struggles - because they help us become better.

When you overcome your struggles, even the ones that are cruel and painful, you will be stronger, wiser, and more grateful. You will develop empathy toward others and use that to help people. Those are the things that matter - what you do for others. None of the material things you and I gather are coming with us when we leave this life. Those will disintegrate into dust.

It's what we do for others.

That's the true gold.

That's why I'm on this mission.

I have a challenge for you - a call to action so that you, too, can experience the gift of giving in its purest form.

Every day for one week, do a good deed for someone without telling anyone. Maybe you donate a few dollars, maybe you buy someone a cup of coffee, or send someone a card or encouraging letter, maybe you mow a neighbor's yard or just tell someone how much you appreciate them. Whatever it is you choose to do, give that gift because you *want* to. Give it wholly and purely, without expecting anything in return. Pay attention to how you feel when you give that gift.

My bet is that you will enjoy the feeling so much you will want to continue experiencing it. And slowly, those around you will notice something different about you without being able to pinpoint what that is. But they will be drawn to your presence. They will appreciate how they feel when they are around you. Eventually you will be leading them by example, without ever saying a word.

Key Takeaways from this Chapter:

1. To whom much is given, much is required.

2. Abundance is everywhere.

3. Giving must be done out of gratitude.

4. We can never out-give God.

5. Send someone a card or encouraging letter.

6. There is power in giving.

7. One of the biggest challenges we have is discovering our motives for our good works.

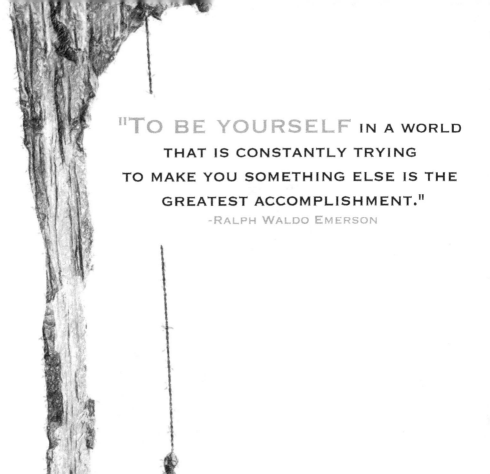

"TO BE YOURSELF IN A WORLD
THAT IS CONSTANTLY TRYING
TO MAKE YOU SOMETHING ELSE IS THE
GREATEST ACCOMPLISHMENT."
-RALPH WALDO EMERSON

...KEEP CLIMBING

Chapter Six

How to Conquer Fear, Doubt, and Anxiety

I want you to be aware of something; The storms of this life are coming. Don't be naive and think that you're going to just coast through a wonderful, successful life. Don't think challenging times are not coming your way, because they are. Maybe you're in those challenging times right now and you believe there is no way out. Maybe you haven't seen the power of God at work flipping realities upside down.

My life has taught me five powerful tools we can use to help us overcome challenging times. These tools helped me and I want to share them with you. Regardless of the size of your bank account; whatever age, race, or gender you are, you can learn how to use these tools to overcome the fear, doubt, and anxiety that often paralyze us into staying in dark places in our lives.

Those five tools are:

- Daily Affirmations
- Reading the Bible
- The Art of Prayer

- Daily or Weekly Journaling
- Professional Counseling

Now, before you roll your eyes and skip this chapter because you are not a religious person, or you don't believe in affirmations, ask yourself why you are reading this book? Most are reading to hear more about my life and to get a glimpse of the journey that brought me to the stage as a performing artist. Some are looking for encouragement and direction, and others, are looking for hope. My goal is not to push my faith on you, but to tell you what has made a difference in my life – and faith is a huge part of that.

There is no easy way to overcome fear, doubt, and anxiety. To find solutions to our problems, we need to have faith; not just faith in ourselves but faith in God. And action. You need to move forward. Remaining stagnant and unmoving in a difficult situation will change nothing. And in some cases, staying there, will make things worse. There is an almost absolute certainty that you will never leave the pit of fear, doubt, and anxiety, if you don't at least try.

I understand what it's like to trust in no one.

I know what it's like to believe that even the Church is not a safe harbor.

I know what it's like to feel stuck in a pit that you will never climb out of.

I also know what it's like to find faith and to find that safe harbor.

I know what it feels like to climb out of the pit and step into the light.

We all go through fear, doubt, and anxiety. It's part of the human condition. Want to know another characteristic of being human? Imperfection. Humans are not perfect. People are going to let us down. It means even people who are "Godly" are going to let you down. That's why having a personal relationship with God is so important, because He always has our best interests at the forefront. He loves us. He cares for us and it is up to us to make sure the foundation of our relationship with Him includes an understanding that He is a good God. We can begin to build that foundation by reading, studying, and attending church.

But what about all the crime, the hate, and the sometimes blatant evil we see or experience firsthand? We live in a fallen world. God gave us a perfect world but He also gave humans free will. The reason we live in a fallen world lies on the human race: our actions and the consequences thereof.

When you start personally experiencing the power of these

five tools, you will unleash a whole new level of awareness and perception that will allow you to do things you never imagined possible.

Daily Affirmations are a method used to talk to yourself in a positive way, on a daily basis. We're constantly flooded with negative thoughts or doubts which are often based in fear. This fear can lead us down rabbit holes that just continue to lead us further and further away from inner peace and positivity. So, in order to combat that, to resist the temptations to be lured down those rabbit holes, we must be diligent about our subconscious thoughts. The more negative things we allow ourselves to focus on, the more those things become negative beliefs about ourselves and those negative beliefs become negative truths. We can flip that script by focusing our thoughts on positive things, even when times are hard.

I've used affirmations in my own life for years and I've personally experienced their impact. I lean strongly on gratitude in my own affirmations. Simply recognizing things that I'm grateful for has had a noticeable impact on me.

When I spiral into discouragement or depression, I flip my emotions by naming things that I am grateful for. These are things within myself and things in my outward life. These are simple habits for everyone to do. Give it a try! Just fill in the blanks in these statements.

I am grateful for _____ in my life.

I am grateful for _____ about myself.

I am grateful for _____ about my family.

Examples from My Daily Affirmations:

*I am grateful for this new day, with new possibilities.

*I am grateful for my talents and abilities.

*I am grateful that I am a kind person.

*I am grateful for the people I have in my life that encourage me to be better.

*I am grateful that I have everything I need to succeed.

Go crazy with your own affirmations!

Go as far as being grateful that you live in a free country where you can wake up, follow a dream, and go after it. And no matter what age you are, if you want to change your life, you can.

When I first began to move in the direction of speed painting and inspirational speaking, I wasn't sure where it was going to lead me. I just knew that I needed to try. I had to trust that I would succeed because I knew it was God's plan for me. In spite of all the things that could go wrong, in spite of how crazy I seemed to people around me, I moved toward my goal. And it has led to where I am today - reaching hundreds of thousands, and soon millions, of people from the stage, with this book, and through continuing to explore new opportunities as God presents them.

Reading the Bible is an experience. The Bible is packed with various forms of holy scripture. Scripture is the inspired Word of God. The scriptures help you build a foundation of faith. You and I have to believe that when we put our feet on the floor, gravity is going to hold us down. That's a foundational truth. Well, scripture is our foundational truth for our spiritual lives. Despite what you may tell yourself or what others say about you, God loves you. Scriptures are sacred writings that guide, encourage, and teach us. They are God's way of speaking his truth in a way we can understand. The Psalms are songs and prayers written for worshiping God. Proverbs give principles, wisdom and direction for daily living.

When I am feeling discouraged, worried, lonely, or . . . lost, I turn to scripture.

The Art Prayer is one extremely important daily practice for me.

Some different types of prayer are meditative prayer, reciting written prayers, or simply having a conversation with

God. The latter is something all of us can do whether we've ever set foot in a church, picked up a Bible, or learned any structured recitation prayers at all. This kind of prayer is more like a heart-to-heart with somebody you trust. I try to look at my relationship with God just the same as any child to a parent. A child asking his Father for the things he needs, or for help or counsel. It is giving our attention to God, where we talk, *but* also listening to Him.

Sometimes our emotions are prayers. Sometimes you can start to pray but you're in such despair that all you can do is cry. That is still a prayer. It's you communicating to God through your emotions. He gave us these emotions for a reason. There may be other times you feel so angry that you are at a loss for words. That's okay, too, because God understands your heart.

Sometimes the most powerful prayers are the silent ones.

I believe it was Buddha who used the expression "monkey mind" to describe the inability to quiet our minds when there are so many thoughts, distractions, and anxieties to contend with. This is where repetitive written prayer can be helpful in order to calm yourself and get focused. When you reach that state of peace, this is when you can have the most powerful conversations with God. You're all in. Present.

However, prayer is not always about asking for something. As I mentioned above, more often than not, it's about listening. If you are in a conversation and more than one person is speaking at once, it's not a conversation at all. It's just an exercise in frustration. If you speak over someone else speaking to you, you won't hear anything. Another example: if I ask you for directions to a restaurant, I have to stop speaking while you are responding to me so I can hear those directions. It's the same thing with prayer. If you are praying for help, and you want to find that help, you have to stop talking long enough to hear the response. Otherwise, you will never find any answers. You'll know when the answer is being given to you if you learn how to listen.

There are probably hundreds of stories in my life where I've overcome fear, doubt, and anxiety through my relationship with God. My whole life has His fingerprints on it. One of the lowest times of my life was when I was overwhelmed with debt. I thought there would be no coming back from that despair. I didn't know where to turn, and I felt myself being pulled down into a pit of doubt and anxiety.

Have you ever felt that way?

This happened in my life, after I'd worked for years to build my business. My wife had supported my dream every step of the way. She'd worked two jobs and never complained about it because she believed in me. We believed that God had a plan for us. That plan was revealed and together we went "all in" making sure we didn't waste the grace that had been bestowed upon us. When Lee came into my life and helped me the way he did, I didn't just sit back and live off his generosity. I worked long days and nights, pouring everything I had into my passion for this dream. Yet, when we achieved success and it seemed like there would be nothing but happiness before us, a shocking and painful betrayal nearly caused financial ruin for us. We had put a family member, who we had helped in the past, in a trusted position in our company and this person stole thousands of dollars from our company (more on this in Chapter 8).

It was daunting to start over. Maybe for you, this moment arrived when you lost your job, or you or someone you love got sick, or maybe you lost someone you loved. Whatever that moment looks like for you, you do not have to live through it alone.

There was nothing left for me to do . . . but pray. I'm not ashamed to say that I was on my knees crying out to God for help and guidance. "Moses moments" are extremely rare. It's highly unlikely there will be a burning bush experience in any of our lives. But it is **not** unlikely that people you know or even total strangers will step forward for God to speak through, to answer prayers. I understand it may be difficult for you to believe I'm not just imagining my relationship with God or to believe that you, too, can have a relationship with Him.

I know you may not even want to. And I want to let you know that whether you know it or not, you already *do* have a relationship with God. Even if you are not listening, He is speaking to you. Even if you don't believe in Him, *He believes in you.*

So why not try talking to Him one day and see how it makes you feel? Why not give yourself the peace and strength of knowing you have an Ally, a Friend, a Father, when it feels like you have no one else in this world? Why not face fear, doubt, and anxiety with the confidence that faith brings, instead of the weight of feeling alone?

If your foundation in faith is strong, you will understand that this earth, this life, is not our true home. Whether it's today or next week, or in five years or 50 years down the road, we're all going to leave this life. If you can put that in your heart and in your mind, it makes it easier to take a full inventory of your life and future.

It's knowing this, that I do what I do. It's why I travel around the country, sometimes doing 12 shows a week, sometimes for 20 people and sometimes for thousands of people. Because while I need to make a living and provide for my family, just like we all do, I also want to give back in a positive way. I not only want to encourage people today, but to encourage generations.

I have overcome everything I have because of my faith in God. I can't hide or deny that.

If there's one thing that I want you to take away from this chapter, it's that you have a Father who loves you and cares for you and wants the best for your life. And He's not going to leave you or forsake you even though you may feel like He has. He wants you to overcome your pain just like I have overcome mine, but He wants you to do it by looking to Him, and not anyone else.

We have to be all in.

We know what anxiety is. We know what fear is. We know what doubt is.

Do we know what to do with them?

The answer is - we give them to God.

The only reason why you and I are still breathing today is that God has planned more for us to do while we are here. I believe that with my whole heart. Whether we are very old or very young, God has a plan for us and a purpose for our lives. We may fulfill that purpose without knowing it and God may call us home. Or we may make decisions that leads us away from that purpose. Whatever life we choose to live and however long we are blessed to live, God will be there at the end of our lives, to welcome us home. Believing this takes faith and trust that it is true.

Daily or Weekly Journaling can also be used as an outlet for seeking to overcome fear, doubt, and anxiety. When we're struggling with these emotions, it can be challenging to understand their underlying causes and patterns. By putting pen to paper, you can begin to sort through your thoughts and feelings, gaining clarity and self-awareness. The process of journaling allows you to confront your fears and doubts directly and serves as a safe space for you to express yourself without fear of judgment. If done consistently, journaling can become an emotional sanctuary where you can freely explore your feelings and reframe negative thought patterns. But it can also be used to track your progress and growth over time. Revisiting past entries reveals the journey of overcoming fear, doubt, and anxiety, highlighting the challenges faced and the strategies that led to positive outcomes. In essence, journaling becomes a powerful tool for personal growth.

Professional Counseling is the last on my list but is the most courageous action I suggest when it comes to overcoming fear, doubt and anxiety. Trained counselors provide a safe and non-judgmental space to explore the root causes of fear and anxiety, helping you gain a deeper understanding of your emotions and triggers. They can also help you identify underlying issues, such as past traumas or negative thought patterns, and help you develop a personalized treatment plan. Counseling offers a compassionate perspective, that can empower you to address your fears, regain control over your life, and cultivate a sense of well-being and resilience.

Key Takeaways from this Chapter:

1. We all experience fear, doubt, and anxiety. And we have options to overcome these challenges with Daily Affirmations, Reading the Bible, Prayer and Professional Counseling.

2. Affirmations are positive statements that help you overcome adversity.

3. Scriptures are sacred writings that guide, encourage, and teach us.

4. Prayer is a heart-to-heart with God.

5. You have a Father in God, who loves you and cares for you, and wants the best for your life.

6. Seeking professional help through a trained professional is a great option in overcoming fear, doubt and anxiety.

PIT (NEGATIVE) THINKING

- **Fearful mindset:** Letting fear hold you back from taking risks or pursuing your dreams.
- **Procrastination:** Delaying action and putting off tasks required to achieve your goals.
- **Self-doubt:** Constantly questioning your abilities and worthiness of success.
- **Negative self-talk:** Engaging in self-criticism and negative inner dialogue.
- **Lack of resilience:** Giving up easily in the face of obstacles or setbacks.
- **Fixed mindset:** Believing that abilities and talents are fixed and cannot be developed or improved.
- **External validation seeking:** Relying solely on others' opinions for validation and approval.
- **Playing the victim:** Blaming external circumstances or others for your lack of progress.
- **Perfectionism:** Setting unrealistically high standards that hinder progress and lead to frustration.
- **Comparison:** Constantly comparing yourself to others and feeling inadequate.

PALACE (POSITIVE) THINKING

- **Faith:** Believing in your ability to learn, grow, and develop new skills. Trusting that God will guide and direct your life, giving you wisdom to make good decisions. Believing in your heart that everything will work out for the best.
- **Self-belief:** Trusting in your capabilities and having confidence in your potential for success.
- **Goal setting:** Setting clear, achievable goals that align with your dreams and aspirations.
- **Positive affirmations:** Practicing positive self-talk and cultivating a positive mindset.
- **Resilience:** Bouncing back from setbacks and using challenges as opportunities for growth.
- **Action-oriented mindset:** Taking consistent, purposeful action towards your goals.
- **Self-motivation:** Cultivating intrinsic motivation and finding inspiration from within.
- **Embracing failure:** Viewing failures as learning opportunities and stepping stones to success.
- **Self-care:** Prioritizing your physical, mental, and emotional well-being to sustain motivation.
- **Gratitude:** Focusing on the positives in your life and being grateful for the opportunities and progress you have.
- **Knowing you are loved:** Even though, maybe at this point you don't believe in God, the fact is, He loves you, believes in you and wants the best for you.

"HE WHO WORKS WITH HIS HANDS IS A LABOURER. HE WHO WORKS WITH HIS HANDS AND HIS HEAD IS A CRAFTSMAN. HE WHO WORKS WITH HIS HANDS AND HIS HEAD AND HIS HEART IS AN ARTIST."
-SAINT FRANCIS OF ASSISI

...KEEP CLIMBING

Chapter Seven

Is That All It Takes?

I think we can all agree that life can be hard. There will be times in your life where you are doing everything right and it feels as though everything is going . . . *wrong*. We've all been there, right? You know, moments like nearly completing a term paper or thesis and your computer glitches and you lose the entire document before you had a chance to save it. Or when you're on your way to a job interview and your car breaks down. Or you have an argument with someone you care about. We all experience stress in varying degrees. It's a normal reaction to the challenges of everyday life.

Whenever I have moments like these - and I have them often - I will admit sometimes takes a lot of effort to catch myself before I let my emotions spiral out of control. When this happens I use another life lesson that I was taught earlier in my career.

It was another busy day for me in my portrait studio. The success I had once craved was here, and there were some days that felt very overwhelming. For me, success meant extremely long hours, with client appointments scheduled so tightly I had to be perfectly "on schedule" all day to make it work. I committed to giving every client my full attention. I went above and beyond in order to make my clients feel like they mattered, and they were special. It was extremely important to me that my studio never felt like a doctor's office, where we all routinely languish in waiting rooms well beyond our scheduled times. It was an incredibly high standard I set for myself - the slightest glitch could send my entire day into a tailspin.

On that particular day, I had back-to-back appointments. That, in itself, wasn't unusual - I always booked clients back-to-back for photo shoots, typically shooting at least eight, 90-minute sessions a day. On this day, though, I had a full schedule of "theater presentations". Rather than simply handling my clients my completed work product, "theater presentations" were my way of making this event extra special for my clients. I set my theater room up with a projector that was pre-loaded with the client's photos. I had specific music queued up and set the lights "just so". I would sit in that room with my clients, listening to the music while their photos played out before them, and savor the emotions this always brought out. I was in my element, doing what I loved. But this day I wasn't feeling that way. In fact, I was feeling like everything was a disaster and I was in the grips of a panic. About halfway through the day's appointments, my projector died and there was not a lot of time before my next time slot. I only had a few precious moments to have everything running smoothly before the client arrived - assuming I could resurrect my projector. So, there I was climbing up and down my ladder, checking wire connections and the outlet, and inspecting the projector to see if anything was broken. With each second that ticked by, my frustration and panic increased. This was magnified when my receptionist told me a non-scheduled client had just popped in and wanted to talk.

Although, I don't encourage drop-ins, I don't actively discourage them. On one hand, I prefer to have order to my day. On the other hand, I strive to serve my clients and make sure they feel appreciated. It just happened that this client popping in was one of the few I had a difficult time connecting with. I couldn't imagine what Marty wanted to talk about.

Marty is a guy a lot of people would call "quirky." He is an inventor who specializes in developing plumbing parts. He has a condition that some would call "flat affect". He doesn't have any emotional expressions or reactions and he speaks in a monotone voice. Previously I had done a commercial photo shoot for him and in spite of my best efforts, I did not succeed in shaking him from his seemingly apathetic state.

Marty is extremely intellectual. So, while his demeanor aligns with someone on high doses of some sort of sedative, what's really happening is his mind is operating on such a higher level than the average person (me) that getting all worked up about anything is a waste of energy for him. He's got better things for his brain to focus on. He also will not shake your hand if you offer it to him. It's the strangest thing to be standing there, hand outstretched and a smile on your face, while he looks right back at you and ignores your hand. Despite these physical tendencies, he is a nice guy. Yet, at this particular moment, I didn't feel like I had the energy, patience, or time for Marty. But he was persistent. He really wanted to talk to me. So, I told my receptionist to send him in and carried on with my efforts to repair the projector. Part of me appreciated knowing he didn't expect a formal greeting and handshake, anyway.

"Hello, Tom," came that familiar flat voice from behind me. I did my best to throw a smile over my shoulder. The projector had the majority of my attention but I put a valiant effort into being friendly, offering him a seat and asking how I could help him. Marty, however, appeared to have forgotten his urgent matter. He was more interested in what I was doing, which only served to fluster me more. Him asking me what I was doing slammed straight into my last nerve, which I worked extremely hard at keeping together while explaining the crisis at hand.

My voice was not monotone, or slow. It was more rapid-fire, borderline hysteria, as I explained my problem. Still for some reason I felt like it was important for me to tell him that I was frustrated, as if he couldn't see or hear that for himself.

"Yeah, I can see that. You do seem really frustrated," he commented. I braced myself for a "Marty-ism". This is when he would elicit advice with the best of intentions. "Tom, how long have you been working on that?" Despite the lack of inflection I knew he was questioning me and expected an answer.

I snapped back at him, no longer even attempting to hide the urgency in my voice, that I'd been working on it for about 20 minutes, and I couldn't get it turned on, and it just broke! My brain was working as fast and haphazardly as my hands. I had no idea what was wrong with the projector and part of me knew that continuing to twist wires and tap on the machine was not solving the problem. The other part of me figured it was better to try anything in the absence of a solution. It was a disaster. The entire day was slipping away from me. I was growing more upset by the moment.

Marty made another monosyllabic comment and I basically exploded in panic and frustration. "I have six more appointments today and these people are all counting on me. Some are driving for hours to get here and I am on a time crunch!" I said all that in one sentence, and one breath.

Marty looked fascinated and bemused at the same time. In all of our other interactions, he'd only seen the Tom who was energetic and well organized. He had never glimpsed the massive preparation and obsessing that went into my work when my clients weren't there. He almost sounded like he was speaking more to himself than to me as he put the pieces together and said, "That's it, then? That's all it takes? The projector goes down and you become this frustrated and get to this level of stress?"

Something about those words made his monotone feel like a lightning bolt. I stopped dead in my tracks, as intrigued by his revelation to me as he was by mine to him. Suddenly it felt more like I was in his office, laying down on a therapist's couch, seeking *his* help. He invited me to take a seat so I could calm down long enough for him to impart his wisdom.

Everything sort of clicked into place for me as he pointed out the futility of frustration dominating my thoughts and actions.

He made me realize the pointlessness of allowing myself to be completely thrown off track just because of a minor glitch in my day. He helped me understand that it's so much harder to find a solution to my challenges if I am not thinking rationally.

Marty's interruption of my frustration and near-panic attack, allowed me to stop and *think*. It prompted enough time for me to step away from the situation long enough to consider replacing the light bulb. Sure enough, the moment I screwed a new bulb in, my projector lit up the room and all was well with the world once again. The disaster I imagined happening . . . never happened at all.

I've never met anyone else like Marty. I've also never forgotten how this meeting with him changed the way I think. To this day, when anything goes wrong, and I am tempted to let frustration or anger take over, I hear Marty's unique voice asking me, "Tom, is that all it takes?" This lesson was a gift. A gift I now give you. I promise that if you use this gift in your life the way I have in mine, it will change things for you. It will allow you to get control of your frustration and fear in challenging or scary moments. It will give you the time you need to work up solutions for you to navigate that moment in ways frustration and fear will not.

Maybe you are being bullied in school or harassed at work. There may be certain behaviors a person does that you cannot control, but what you *can* control is how you allow that person to impact your emotions. The next time that person does whatever it is they are doing to you and you find yourself thinking about them with a feeling of dread, fear, self-loathing, or hopelessness - ask yourself these questions: Is that all it takes? Are you going to allow this person to determine how the rest of your day goes? Or how the rest of your life goes?

I can't talk about fear, doubt, or anxiety, and not talk about social media. In my opinion, social media is one of the biggest causes of anxiety and depression. We all scroll and see things happening in other people's lives. Or, at least we see what they want us to see. Maybe if things are going well for us that day we are happy for others who are smiling or celebrating something in their lives. But what about the days where we are already depressed and hurting? The days we mistakenly seek a reason to be happy through social media, and instead all we see is everyone else being happy? Is that all it takes to make you sink lower? Or are you able to recognize that you are the one who gets to decide that? When you frame things with that perspective, you realize how little power people really do have over you.

My wife and I even use this in our marriage. When I get myself stressed out over something, Karen asks me, "Tom, is that all it takes?" And then we laugh together. That one simple question has diffused an innumerable amount of situations.

Now, this doesn't mean every source of stress can be magically eliminated with this strategy. There are definitely times when the answer to that question is . . . **yes!** Yes, there are some events in life that are powerful enough to derail our day, or our week, and potentially the rest of our lives. When these events happen, it's okay to let yourself feel whatever you are feeling - you just have to make sure you don't let those feelings become permanent.

The way you respond to stress makes a big difference.

There is another part to this lesson.

I've shared with you how asking yourself "Is that all it takes?" can help you recover from a situation. Now it's important to understand how one decision could have a disastrous impact on you.

Remember earlier in the BIG acronym, when I talked about the individuals you choose to hang around?

There is a story I share during some of my shows. It's a true story about five teenage boys. Rather than use their real names I'm going to call them Liam, Noah, Oliver, Elijah, and James. Now, up to this point the group of 15-year-olds had never been in any trouble with the law. Oliver and Elijah were "A" students; Noah was the captain of his Junior Varsity Basketball team; Liam was on his school's chess team; and James was obsessed with dirt bikes. As typical teens, they would get bored and fool around, but had never crossed the line of committing an actual crime.

Until they did.

The day started out as any other day. The boys were hanging out in Liam's basement playing video games. After a while, they got bored. Not sure what to do, they all started to throw out ideas. Noah half-joked that they should go rob someone. The other boys laughed, not taking Noah seriously, and came up with mock scenarios of what they would do, each scenario more ridiculous than the last. Interrupting the laughter, Noah said, "No, seriously man. I know a guy . . . my brother hangs with him, I think he's a plug. He's always carrying around a fat knot." Sobering, the conversation turned more serious. As the enthusiasm grew amongst them, Noah sent a text to have the dealer meet them in the local Walmart parking lot.

Before any of them really knew what was happening, Noah was driving them to Walmart. As he drove, Noah was throwing out a plan for all of them. Liam, who sat in the passenger seat, was laughing with James who sat in the backseat.

Oliver and Elijah were quiet and nervous, hoping someone else would point out that this was a stupid idea.

But no one did.

At the designated time, the car pulled up. As the dealer rounded the front of his car, the five teenagers jumped out of the car and started beating him.

Somehow, the man being beaten withstood the cruel kicks and punches, managing to break free from the group. The teenagers watched their victim run to his car. They made the decision to get back in their car and flee the scene - but suddenly it was they who were being hunted. Their victim hadn't run to his car to escape. No - he was furious. And he had a gun. The teenagers were yelling and their hearts were pounding as they screamed at Liam to get them out of there. Bullets sprayed the car and crashed through the windows.

It wasn't a game anymore. It wasn't the adventure they'd thought it would be. They weren't prepared for this turn of events.

Their car screeched into the parking lot of a small convenience store and the boys almost fell over one another in their rush to get out and take stock of things.

"Can you believe that? That guy shot at us!" James yelled, his adrenaline racing through his veins. The incredulous, excited voices quieted just a brief moment later.

Only three of them had jumped out of the car.

The other two had not. Horrified, the three boys realized Oliver and Elijah had been shot and killed.

Less than an hour before, they had been five teenage boys just hanging out. They had futures to step into. They had sunrises to see and storms to weather. They had heartbeats to feel and challenges to overcome, and gifts to discover and share with the world. And all it took to end those two lives was one decision. A joke that led to a decision. One person to not speak up and point out how foolish it was.

The man they attacked, and who shot at them, went to prison for 20 years. Noah, James, and Liam were sentenced to 10 years in prison. But it's not the walls they were sent to live behind that were their true consequence. It was the pain and guilt of knowing the choice they made ended their friends' lives.

One question or one decision has the potential to change your life.

When things aren't working out or going the way you want them to. Ask yourself this simple question. ***Is that all it takes?*** Sometimes when you do this, you're able to operate in a different paradigm and things begin to shift and change regarding your approach to the problem. You may even notice a way out or through the situation at hand.

Try it the next time one of these things happen to you:

When people have let you down…

When you don't make the team or get that job…

When your business goes through a rough patch…

When you get a bad grade or fail a test…

When you have a health scare…

When your car breakdown…

the list goes on and on...

Asking the question **Is that all it takes?** should put us in a healthier state of mind. We shift away from being scared and depressed, over to a space of thinking of answers or solutions to the problem. Ultimately, we start to believe 'This isn't going to break me. This isn't going to keep me down. I have options.' I'm going to work through this situation and rise victoriously.

Key Takeaways from this Chapter:

1. Reacting to a crisis with frustration and fear creates a bigger crisis.

2. You are one decision away from changing your life.

3. You are the only one who determines what you will make of your life.

4. You are stronger than you may realize.

"GIVE ME SIX HOURS TO CHOP DOWN A TREE AND I WILL SPEND THE FIRST FOUR SHARPENING THE AXE."
-ABRAHAM LINCOLN

...KEEP CLIMBING

FROM THE PIT TO THE PALACE 157

Chapter Eight

The Beginning

Up to this point, I've spent quite a lot of time talking about my journey as a portrait photographer. One of the questions I receive most is how I transitioned from photography to becoming a speed painter and inspirational speaker.

With every success story, there is a beginning.

Have you ever had something so random and unexpected happen to you, that it's impossible to predict how you are going to react? I feel like that is a common theme in my life. Good things, bad things, scary things, exciting things - the majority of the significant events that affect my life in one way or another have a way of catching me off guard.

One such event began with a random phone call from a friend. This friend happened to be the mayor of my town. He didn't waste time with small talk and got straight to the point. "Tom, we want you to be a City Councilor," he stated in the same way someone would say, "Hey, let's go out to eat tonight." I was sure I'd either misheard him or he was joking. I went with the joking option first.

He wasn't joking.

A sudden vacancy left a town councilman position needing to be filled. Normally this was an elected position, but in circumstances like this, the mayor can appoint a replacement until the next scheduled election. Apparently, he'd decided *I* was that replacement.

I can think of few things I wanted less to do with than politics. The very thought of becoming a politician at any level is about as far from my nature and vision for my life as, say, being a lion tamer.

In hindsight, I should have taken my chances with the lions.

Still, my distaste for his request was countered by a sense of duty and, perhaps, obligation. Unsurprisingly, my wife shared that sense of duty. The town, as a community, had supported our business in so many ways and we both agreed it would be wrong to refuse this request. Up to this point, I had a vague understanding of the responsibilities of a councilman so I began to research the role and to prepare for serving in this position to the best of my ability.

I joined six other town councilmen, who, for some reason, willingly stayed and even campaigned for these jobs. For me, it was a nightmare from start to finish. Almost overnight, I had people hating me. Clients who had sung my praises as a photographer now viewed me as an enemy because they hated the mayor, and *he* had appointed me. Therefore, they now felt compelled to hate me, too. People I had always viewed as normal, kind, hard-working, and compassionate - underwent some sort of ugly transformation when they stepped through the door on Councilman night. You know how some people are as sweet as pie in person but then rude when they drive - leaning on their horns, tailgating, cutting other drivers off, cursing, and all that? Well, that's pretty much the same thing that happens to people when they step through the Looking Glass at Councilman Night.

It was shocking and uncomfortable to be screamed at.

I am a non-confrontational person by nature. The energy of those meetings left me totally drained and in need of spiritual comfort. They made me miss my father even more. Since his passing a few years prior, I'd always felt a void. But in times like this, it felt like that void was swallowing me whole. And after a few of those open microphone nights, I almost wished it would. I know now, if he'd been alive my dad would have advised me *not* to take the position. There were many nights I left those meetings and went to the cemetery to visit my father's grave instead of bringing that toxic energy home to my family. We had two little girls by then. Neither they, nor my wife, deserved to feel a shred of the negativity that clung to me after those encounters with the public.

The only consolation I had was that I knew I was making a difference for the people I represented.

I was serving the largest ward (also the lowest income ward), of my city. Among the homeless population in that ward was a depressingly high number of veterans. I was proud to be a part of creating low-income housing for these veterans. The homes we created were brand new then, and they're still in good condition today.

Highlights like these got me through those two and a half years as a Councilman, but the cost of that service was still too high. It jaded me so much, I not only celebrated being done with it, I convinced my wife to put as much distance between us and that experience as possible.

HAVE I MENTIONED THAT MY WIFE, KAREN, IS A SAINT? WELL, MAYBE NOT A CANONIZED SAINT WITHIN THE CHURCH, BUT SHE'S A SAINT TO ME.

Never mind that my business and clientele were still in New York or that we were in the midst of a housing market crash. We still didn't let any of the obstacles stop us. We sold our New York house and moved into a rental apartment in Florida within a month. A year later, our hard work paid off and we managed to buy our dream house.

While our family adjusted to our new surroundings, I spent much of the time commuting to New York. All of my income flowed from my studio there. For two weeks a month I would shoot over a hundred sessions, then return to Florida while a family member managed my New York studio. There were a lot of moving parts but we were confident it would all work out.

Until it went terribly wrong.

Do you remember in Chapter Six when I mentioned the trusted family member who stole from us?

Karen and I noticed discrepancies long before it became

impossible to ignore. We just couldn't bring ourselves to believe there was more to the red flags than a perfectly good explanation. So, while my gut was warning me that something was terribly wrong, my brain was protecting me from the hurt as best it could. The income was coming in, the problem was, our statements were not changing. It didn't make sense to us. Even when clients began asking me why the studio manager was scheduling meetings in parking lots and requesting they pay cash for their photos, part of us desperately wanted to believe that the credit card machines really *were* broken. This was unfathomable to me. The longtime vision of my studio was to serve our clients to the upmost. Giving them the *best* experience, start to finish.

My father and Lee had both passed away - both would probably have knocked some sense into me long before I finally acknowledged the problem. But in their absence, I allowed myself to avoid a confrontation far longer than I should have.

It was a costly mistake. Most of the time leadership is uncomfortable. It's just a fact of business and life.

I had to confront this family member. The amount she had stolen over the years was substantial. It was a crushing blow both financially and emotionally. It literally brought me to my knees. I had to stand in our dream home, look at my beautiful family, and tell them we could no longer afford to stay in Florida. We would have to return to New York and start over. It was one of the most humbling experiences of my life.

My daughters were teenagers. This could have been very messy, emotionally, for them. But they have their mother's grace and were able to look on the positive side of things. So, we moved from our dream home, back to New York into an apartment we had yet to see. When we did step into that disgusting space with its pet-stained carpets, I felt like I was stepping right back into the pit I thought I'd climbed out of. Even worse - it felt like I'd thrown my family in there with me.

I felt depression tightening its grip on me.

Have you ever experienced a similar moment in time? A moment when everything you worked so hard for was yanked right out from underneath you and things felt so overwhelming? Are you going through a moment like that right now?

Have you even considered what you would do if something like this happened to you? Whatever the answer to those questions is, I promise you adversity makes you stronger, if you have faith and push through it. I know this because I lived it. I know this because I know so many other people who have as well, and you know what? We are all better and stronger people because of it.

You will be too.

One of the first things you can do (besides to pray, and maybe even read some Scriptures) is to let humility in.

Accept the fact that pride, or a sense of it, will only hurt you right now. Then, ask for help.

For me, this meant going to the bank. In addition to paying rent on that miserable apartment, I still owned the building where my photography studio was located. Above the studio was an outdated apartment. After many hours of discussion and prayer, Karen and I decided to renovate the apartment for our family to live in. I knew I was going to need another loan to help me meet monthly expenses and climb out of this pit. So, I went and sat down with the owner of our local bank, Tom Clark. I humbled myself and confided my situation to him. Mr. Clark had known me for a long time and he knew I was a hard worker. He knew I did what I could to give back to the community and something in him was able to ignore all the reasons *not* to give me a loan. "Get your life back on track with this," he said.

So, I got to work.

Remember all those friends I had back when Lee came into my life? When my phone constantly rang with friends and family wanting to get together with me? Well, my phone wasn't ringing with friends anymore. At least, not after the first day of gutting the apartment over my studio. Seven friends answered my call that day. After that first day, my friends Bobby, Dan, Dave and Steve remained on the project with me. However, life gets busy and soon after it was just Dan Breckenridge and I. He and I became close friends working on that apartment. It was grueling work. After several months, despite our best efforts, progress was slow. So, I made another call to ask two more close friends, Nick and Angelo Carletta, who also happened to be contractors, for help. They agreed to take over the remainder of the project and for the next four months helped me complete the renovation of the apartment.

It felt like a victory when my family moved into this apartment. Although, there was too much work to do to stop and celebrate.

Times had changed. Technology was evolving and the better camera phones got, the less portrait bookings I received at the studio. It wasn't the first time I had to grow and change with the tide of technology, nor would it be the last. I went after the work and faced the challenges ahead of me, but I had to finally admit to myself, that it wasn't as much fun this time around. It was like putting a bandaid on a gaping wound. The work and the effort were not sustainable. This was not an appropriate dressing for the wounds that had been inflicted upon me. It felt like no matter how hard I worked, nothing *worked* - you know what I mean?

In times like this, I am always more grateful I have my faith to turn to.

"Lord," I prayed, "What am I going to do here? How do I change this all around?" All I could do at that point was continue putting my best effort in and trusting the Lord would provide me an opportunity to overcome this - if I didn't give up. I knew He could flip it all around.

When I think back to this time and remember how lost and defeated I felt, I am filled with renewed wonder at the mysterious ways God works. I could never have imagined then, that all of what I was going through was not intended to derail me, but to guide me to the exact place I needed to be, in order to step through the door God was about to open for me.

That door happened to open at a Best Buy store.

Errands are typically unexciting. We have a list of things

to buy or pay or drop off or pick up. We make the rounds, and we get on with our day, right? At least that's how my errands usually go. But one day not long after I had prayed for some help and direction, I ran into an old client of mine at Best Buy. He recognized me first and caught my attention. We did the back and forth banter to catch up before he asked me a strange question. "Tom, have you ever painted portraits before?" Painting was not something I had ever tried and, honestly, I had never been interested in it. "I wear a tuxedo to my weddings," I laughed. "I don't like being dirty and covered in paint." Remembering this moment and how I once felt about painting amuses me now.

I wonder how many gifts we all have within us that we never open?

Fortunately for me, this former client appeared in my life to help me discover mine. He had a video queued up on his phone. An artist named Denny Dent. In the video, Denny appeared to be in his fifties, he was painting really fast, with his hands and brushes, to loud rock and roll music. He even had paint splatter in his hair from throwing so much paint. I'd never seen anyone paint like that before.

It was mesmerizing.

In that moment, right there, I knew this is what I was destined to do.

It was as clear to me as a blazing hot sun in a clear blue sky. Again, I had never painted before. So this was crazy, right? But using the same passion I had when I picked up my camera, the same certainty and drive that led me to become a photographer - led me to become a painter. I put my blinders on, seeing only the vision of myself painting like Denny in the video I had watched.

Only differently. My way.

All I had to do now was tell my family and, of course, learn how to become an extraordinary artist. I kept this revelation to myself the first night. I had preparations to make. The next night at the dinner table, I told my girls to come downstairs with me - I had something to show them. I led my family into the studio and seated them in front of an easel I'd placed a large blank canvas on. I was so fired up. I couldn't wait to share this new passion with the people I am most passionate about on this earth. I felt the inspirational music I'd selected wash through me, took a deep breath, and let the emotion guide my hands up and down and back and forth, paint was splashing in my hair off of the canvas and onto my clothes and on the floor. I was completely lost in the moment. I flipped the painting over to reveal the masterpiece I had painted, then stepped back.

One look at the girls' faces and my stomach sank.

My daughters were staring at me as if I'd lost my mind. My wife was already trying to figure out how to let me down gently. The portrait on the canvas looked nothing like the portrait of Einstein I'd envisioned. The silence was worse than if they'd outright "booed" me. Karen cautiously approached the canvas and her husband, clearly wondering if he had completely separated from reality. She started offering constructive criticism - "Maybe if you did this . . . ."

As far as epic fails go, this was a pretty big one.

This is the part of my story that I want you to pay extra attention to.

Because I know you've had moments like that, too. And if you haven't yet - trust me, you will. Actually, we will all have these moments, probably more than once. So, *if* these moments will happen, is not the question. The question is, *how will you respond when they do?*

It would have been perfectly acceptable for me to hang my head in embarrassment and never try to be a painting artist again. My family would eventually have forgotten all about it - but I would not have. I know I would never have stopped wondering . . . *what if?* What if I had tried again? What if I had not given up?

Regret is worse than failure.

The regret of abandoned dreams and roads not taken, the *"what ifs"* in life will hurt you far more than the epic disasters will.

For the next four months I worked during the day at my portrait studio, then painted in the evenings. This is why it's so important to pursue whatever it is that you are passionate about, even when things don't seem to be going your way. You may have to do what I did and work during the day, while you work at night, following a new dream. It won't be easy, so this is what separates the people who climb out of their pit life from those who do not. Don't get me wrong, it was exhausting. I squeezed family time in wherever I could, but I was determined.

The beautiful portrait studio I had so painstakingly created was now covered in paint splatter. It was on the walls, the floor, and the ceiling. With every stroke of my brush I was stepping further away from the past, and into my new purpose.

Unfortunately, I had to pay to walk that path. That meant I couldn't completely destroy the room that I still earned an income from. My solution seemed perfectly logical to me. Our historic, 100-year-old building had a basement. We never went down into the cobweb-infested, musty space. The spider population was thriving and we had previously chosen to let them enjoy their space unbothered, like the benevolent landlords we were.

All dreams require sacrifice.

I was certainly sacrificing. My family was, too. And now it was time for the spiders to sacrifice their peace and quiet in the name of progress. My friend Angelo Carletta is a rock-solid, supportive friend. Angelo was not only a great friend, he is a highly skilled contractor, as well. He answered my call for help yet again and didn't flinch when I told him I wanted to excavate the basement floor to create a painting pit I could practice my craft in. Angelo is what I call a foxhole friend. I can call him any time, day or night and he would simply say, "How can I help?"

Do you have people in your life like that? If you do, cherish them. It's rare.

Angelo and I went to work with picks and shovels. The two of us pulled four tons of dirt out of that basement, one bucket at a time. He had a trailer we dumped each bucket of dirt on. He then delivered that dirt to customers who used it for their own projects, reminding me of the exponential good that acts of kindness can have. After the pit was dug out, Angelo poured concrete. He then added in a set of stairs and my painting pit was finished.

One of the many things I love about Karen is that she always believes in me. If I'm going after something and my heart is all in it, any worry she feels is outweighed by her love for me and her understanding that I have to do what I feel called to do. Her faith and trust never questions mine.

I know I am talking a lot about climbing *out* of a pit. So it may seem weird that I went to such extremes to *build* a pit.

But in this case my pit was also my palace.

Everything is relative.

I spent three more months down in the basement, lost in the wonder of my new passion. The pit was perfect - I could be as messy as I wanted to be with no worries. I created a wooden platform, and I put it on a spinner. I found an engineer, Lou Gonzalez, who designed it so I could spin the "canvas" as I painted, which was really just a board with a huge sheet of construction paper on it. It was pretty amazing. Finally the day arrived when I was ready to perform for my family one more time.

My daughters reluctantly came down the basement steps.

"Dad, this is *annoying. It doesn't come out the way you think it does, Dad!"

Karen jumped in like she always does, encouraging the girls to give it a chance and showing me she had my back. Meanwhile, she was probably bracing herself for another train wreck, too. With the girls all seated, I turned the music on and let my hands start flying around the canvas one more time. I felt Einstein come to life on my canvas, and when I flipped it over for the final presentation, my family once again sat in stunned silence.

This time, though, the silence was different.

Karen had tears streaming down her gorgeous face as she walked over to me. Squeezing me tight, she told me I had just taught our daughters that if you put your heart into whatever you do, you can do anything your heart believes in.

I've performed on thousands of stages over the years, for hundreds of thousands of people. I've wept and laughed and left my sweat and heart on stages all over the country.

But no performance was more important to me than the one in my studio that day.

That performance for my girls took the fire burning in me and poured lighter fluid on it. I was burning with inspiration and a need to take this to the next level. I just didn't know where to start. You'll remember me mentioning the past client who approached me at Best Buy that long ago day? Well, he just so happened to work in the entertainment industry. For privacy's sake, we'll call him "John". John offered to be my agent, telling me that once I got some experience he could book me for paid performances.

I thought that sounded pretty good. I just had to figure out where I would get that experience. You see how this whole part of my life didn't just come together at once? How I didn't have all the answers to my questions in advance? I just had to have faith that the answers would come to me when the time was right. I had to focus on what was right in front of me without worrying about what was around that next turn. I had to be wholly present in every step I took as I walked this path.

I knew I had a special talent but who did I want to use it to help? What was my purpose? Who do I want to paint? What is my message? And who are the people who need to hear it? How do I get booked to perform for them?

While I searched for answers to all those questions, I focused on the ones I could answer first. And thanks to having followed my friend Lee's instructions to give back in a way that does not involve a lot of money, I had an answer to where I would perform, and for whom. Lee's challenge inspired me to take something I love doing and use it as a way to give back. I've always loved basketball. I'm not very good at it but I don't care. I still love it. So I called the athletic director of the local high school and booked the high school gym every Sunday night. I had to go to the school, fill out paperwork, get an insurance policy, and other things that were tedious but necessary to put my plan in motion.

My friend Tom Pasternak and I, put the word out that on Sunday nights the gym was open to any young men aged 16 and up, to come play some basketball for free. The only condition was that before we played we would do a 10-minute devotional. These young men also had to check their emotions and pride at the door because we weren't going to tolerate cursing and fighting and all the garbage they picked up out there on the streets.

It started slowly. For the first year we had about 15 guys show up every week. They loved it and looked forward to it as much as we did. The next year more people came, and we kept growing until it wasn't unusual to have 50 or more people there every week. These guys were just soaking it all up; the prayer, the faith, and playing basketball.

This is where I first developed the confidence to speak in front of people.

I was learning my purpose and God was honing my skills so I could accomplish it.

The program was going strong at the time I launched my painting career. I stacked that up against my new calling and realized how this program could intertwine with my painting. I have this painting talent. I have something to say and I'm going to combine the two. Then I'm going to bring this program into schools and colleges around the country. The "G" goals in my B.I.G. strategy started to come alive!

And that's what I set out to do.

My first audience was the basketball group.

One Sunday night, instead of our normal routine, I painted a portrait of Jesus for the guys at the basketball program.

Now, remember, some of these guys who came to this program lived hard lives. Some of them we met throughout the years had spent time in prison. We'd have some of the men coming in stoned or high. It was surreal to see these former (and sometimes current) criminals, drug users and drug dealers, some of whom were violent, all come into this gym and leave those troubled lifestyles outside for five hours every week. It was a sheer testament to the power of faith and the good within all of us that moved so many of those young men to use that experience as a stepping stone to turn lives around for the good.

And here I was, this high energy, non-confrontational guy, sometimes pointing at these men and kicking them out of the gym for cursing or fighting. Some were expelled for a full month before being allowed to return to the program.

Many years later, I would see some of these guys, and where they were in their current lives. One young man's story in particular has stuck with me. My wife and I were at Macy's. I was standing in the women's department, holding her clothes on my shoulder, waiting for her to do her shopping.

All of a sudden this guy comes up to my wife and introduces himself. Then he approaches me and says, "Tom, my name is Mike. Do you remember me from the basketball program?" I did remember and told him so. I remembered having to kick him out once or twice.

He then went on to tell my wife and I about how that program changed his life.

He told us how it inspired him to get off drugs, and to build a career. He even introduced us to his wife and daughter who were there with him. I started to choke up. Mike had tears of joy in his eyes.

He gave me a hug and said goodbye, and I can still feel the power of that hug today, and I believe I will carry that power with me forever.

I hadn't really known what the impact of that program would be when I started it. But I did know that if I achieved nothing else in my life other than to help one person like Mike, it was all worth it. I'm so glad Karen was there for that moment, too. It was no small thing for us to give up every Sunday night as a family. It was no small thing for my family to support that program. So, for Karen to experience that moment with me and Mike was a complete blessing.

That's the kind of program this was. Yes, it was about basketball and yes, we played hard and we loved it. But it was also about addressing some really hard issues. It was about working together as a group to help one another get our lives on track.

Performing and painting for this group was a perfect fit.

School administrators started hearing about the performances and they started booking me to perform for their students. I had done the work I needed to do, to launch my painting and speaking career. My agent had somehow sensed this potential way back in that Best Buy. His crafty mind was already spinning long before I had that spinning wheel in my painting pit, long before I had the slightest clue how to do any of this. He knew if I learned this craft, and trusted him, he could book me out around the country and take a piece of the pie.

Well, I put the work in and I learned the craft. I put my whole heart into this endeavor and "John" started booking me to perform in colleges. The bookings began to multiply and it quickly became apparent that I could make a living doing this. Unfortunately, my agent wasn't the ethical partner I'd envisioned for this adventure. Just when things seemed like they'd all come together, I got a little surprise. One afternoon I was emailed a 17-page contract and he called to tell me I **had** to sign it within the next **three** hours.

All sorts of alarms were sounding in my head. I didn't even understand half of what was written on those documents. I went straight to my attorney. He read it through in front of me and said, "We're not signing this." John wanted 50% of everything I made for the next five years. He was also demanding that I re-sign with him after those five years or there would be penalties and legal fees.

I was in total shock. Mind you, I'm a businessman and I understand his need for a commission - it's common sense. But I could not believe he was demanding such a high return and the non-negotiable terms.

With Karen by my side, I picked up the phone and called him saying, "I am not signing this, John." He went **nuts**. Screaming. Cursing. Through it all he continued attempting to bully me into signing his contract.

We knew right then and there that I would have to find a new agent moving forward.

So, once again, I was forced to prove to myself how much I really wanted this new career.

Was this obstacle going to make me give up? *("Is that all it takes, Tom?")*

Heck no.

There was no time to be stressed or to let doubt creep in. I knew I was on the right path and I knew doors would open if I kept knocking.

And sure enough, they did. I was working hard and learning the business. With the help of my new found agents, I began to fill my calendar once again, and with each performance I was able to shape what kind of performer I wanted to be.

I was still learning the business in many ways. Then, COVID-19 really knocked me down, like it did to so many other people and businesses. It was extremely difficult when you build your entire business and income around a model that requires public gatherings, and then public gatherings are banned for almost two years. It was devastating.

Once again I was faced with a test of my will and my faith. Did I really want to continue on this path? Did I really believe it would all be okay again?

I did.

I just had to find a way to hold on until things opened back up and my business picked back up. The COVID pandemic was a hard time for humanity. Many people are still struggling to recover from those years. Maybe you are one of them. Maybe you lost someone you love. Maybe you got sick and still haven't fully recovered. Maybe the isolation sent you into a depression you still struggle with. Or maybe you were able to use that time at home to learn a new skill, to work on yourself becoming stronger and smarter. Maybe you prayed more. Maybe you started taking care of yourself more, eating better and started exercising.

Maybe you discovered a whole new passion.

Whatever your life looks like today, however it's changed in the past few years, you have a choice just like I did. Just like we all do - are you going to live your dreams, no matter how hard it is to build them, or are you going to stay in your own pit of unfulfilled purpose?

We talked about fear earlier in this book, but it's worth repeating; Fear can paralyze you. If you get stuck in that pit of fear, you won't make any moves towards your dreams. You won't want to grow and try new things. Fear will take over and keep you down for the count. For me, my faith helped me win that fight. I started this whole venture through much time in prayer. I have prayed every step of the way since, including good times and bad times. When challenges looked like they were going to be insurmountable I silently uttered, "Lord, now what?" "Please, show me the way." And then one thing would lead to another. I would continue keeping my eyes open, looking for signs or lessons or opportunities, and the Lord would always send them to me.

I would see these signs everywhere.

If you or I are not moving forward, we're
regressing. There's no middle ground.

My life continues to move forward in ways I could never have imagined. This would be impossible without having faith.

Our daughter Jordynn thought I was absolutely crazy when she saw me paint my first painting. Today, she works with me. She has seen me in some of the worst and hardest times in my life. I love that she now gets to be a part of some of my most incredible moments, coming with me to my performances. She's now meeting new people and is a huge help at our events. I am excited to be on this journey with her. Together we're making memories. Together we're making a difference in the lives of others.

Your life matters! Keep fighting and going after your dreams. *Don't give up!* You too have memories to make with the people you care most about.

Key Takeaways from this Chapter:

1. Ask a lot of questions before you jump into something. Do the research and make sure you understand what someone is asking of you, before you commit to saying yes.

2. The things that we are in despair over can dig us deeper into a pit fear and isolation. Use the challenges that are in your life as a ladder or as a strong rope to help you climb up out of the darkness.

Some of the guys from Sunday Night Basketball program.

"IF YOU JUDGE PEOPLE,
YOU HAVE NO TIME TO LOVE THEM."
-MOTHER TERESA

...KEEP CLIMBING

Chapter Nine
Bullies Suck

I said it.

We all know it - even those of us who are or have been bullies, ourselves. Whether you are a victim of bullying or you are the bully, you have been hurt. It's not unusual to discover that some of the worst bullies are experiencing some level of trauma in their own lives. When that trauma or stress overpowers resiliency, it is channeled into negative behavior. Some people hurt themselves. Others lash out at people around them.

Bullies stop bullying in one of two ways: They heal their emotional pain, or they are defeated by someone else.

I like to think the people who bullied me have healed their wounds - even the kids who beat me up when I was just eight years old. I'm not sure whose idea it was for me to spend the day alone at our city pool. I just remember it was a steamy hot summer day when my uncle dropped me off. I was just a little eight-year-old kid being dropped off all by myself at a gigantic pool, packed with hundreds of people I didn't know. Old people, young people, people of all races and backgrounds. One thing we all had in common is we all felt the summer heat.

The parking lot was packed. The pool was even more packed. There were so many people in the pool we could only stand because there was not enough room for us to swim. It seemed like everyone else there was there with a friend or a group. Some were bussed in from the city. Others carpooled or rode their bikes together or got dropped off with friends.

The hours passed without me saying a word to anyone. Occasionally the pool would empty in shifts long enough to swim. I took advantage of those moments to splash around, partially enjoying it and partially just trying to pretend I was enjoying it. I was used to being lonely at home.

But being lonely while surrounded by hundreds of people is harder, you know?

Finally it was almost time for my uncle to pick me up. I hopped out of the pool, dried off, and headed toward the recreation building. Leaning in the doorway I watched people having fun. They were playing ping pong and all sorts of games. Suddenly, out of nowhere, something hit me hard in my stomach. I was so confused. It hurt so much. What could it have been? Before I could process any of it another blow knocked me to the ground. In the swirl of pain and confusion I could see several pairs of feet in a circle around me. It was a group of kids I did not know, and they were kicking me as hard as they could.

The attack was vicious and terrifying.

I was so scared it was hard to breathe because of the pain. Who were they? Why were they doing this?

Wham! A foot kicked my head.

Wham! Another foot kicked me in my side at the same time.

Over and over the kicks came for what felt like an eternity but was probably just a couple of minutes.

No one came to my rescue.

No one stopped them.

I tried as best as I could to protect myself, to cover my face and head. I tucked into a ball and still the kicks continued.

Finally, it ended as suddenly as it began. They all walked away without saying anything to me. I had no clue who they were or why they attacked me.

So there I was, just an eight-year-old boy, alone, terrified, and traumatized. I was surrounded by people but may as well have been invisible.

I wasn't bleeding.

There were no visible wounds for anyone to see.

But my whole body hurt and it felt like they had kicked every inch of me. Even worse than that, my heart hurt. I was so devastated that people would see me and decide they wanted to hurt me. I could not understand why.

Why would anyone want to hurt me? Did they have any idea what they'd done to me? Even more than the physical pain? Did they understand the sheer terror I felt? Did they know I would have nightmares about this, and I would be afraid to come back here?

Did they care?

I shuffled out to the parking lot in time to see my uncle arrive. The shock had such a grip on me that I couldn't bring myself to tell him what happened. My uncle didn't dig deeply into asking me how I was, either, so I was able to just sit there in silence.

I never told anyone about that day.

What was the point?

That was my first real experience with bullying; the randomness and the cruelty.

My eight-year-old brain couldn't look at the whole picture, but I know today that those kids who did that to me had to have been hurting. They had to have been living lives where they felt powerless, scared, or traumatized themselves. Maybe none of them would do something like that on their own. Maybe it was the power of the mob mentality that made it seem like a good idea. Kind of like the story I shared about the five teenagers who decided to rob someone. Maybe it was just a bad idea that no one felt courageous enough to protest.

I know it's hard to feel compassion for someone who is hurting you. I also know it's possible to be angry, afraid, and even a little vengeful yet still feel some level of compassion for that person or those people.

It's important to understand that the people bullying you are in pain.

They're frustrated. They're upset. Probably not with you personally - they're most likely upset about something else going on in their lives.

That doesn't make it acceptable to be a bully.

When I travel the country speaking to students, I always talk about bullying.

One time I surprised myself as much as everyone else when something moved me to flip the script. At the beginning of the assembly, I looked out at the hundreds of young faces staring back at me and said, "If you are a bully, I want to see you up here on stage after the show."

I repeated my request again at the end of the show. I challenged them to have the courage to come on stage.

Sure enough, at the end of the performance, a teacher escorted a student on stage to see me. He looked like he was in the eighth grade, or thereabout. His name was "Andy" the teacher informed me, and he wanted to speak to me.

With the teacher remaining at Andy's side, I gave him a hello and did my best to appear inviting so he would feel comfortable speaking. Clearly there was something he felt a need to unburden himself from, or he wouldn't be there.

"Mr. Varano," he said, "I'm a bully and I don't even know why I do it." The sincerity in his voice came through loud and clear. It took courage for him to come talk to me, and I told him so. I also knew why he was being a bully. Andy accepted my invitation to sit down right there on the stage floor, his teacher nearby, as I asked him about his home life. His answer didn't surprise me but it did make my heart ache for him. Andy's father had been into drugs, and that had landed him in jail. He had never met his mom and he lived with his grandparents.

"You're hurting," I told him. "You're frustrated and angry, and that's why you're bullying. You're taking your pain out on kids who don't deserve it. Can you see that?"

Andy could have gotten angry at me and walked away when I said this to him. But his heart had been so hurt for so long, he was ready to listen. Andy admitted he did see that and he told me he just didn't know what to do about any of it.

As I started to respond to Andy, another student came up on stage, walked over to me and sort of whispered in my ear, "Mr. Varano, great show! But, um, I've tried to commit suicide three times this month."

Now that's quite a statement to process. If I ever needed proof that I reach these kids when I perform and speak for them, here it was. I wanted to help this young man with his very serious problem. I also wanted to help Andy, so I told this boy to wait a little bit, and I would speak with him, too. I know I am only in these students' lives for a few precious heartbeats. Their pain and their challenges will be with them long after I am on another stage, in another town, speaking to other students. So I motioned Andy's teacher back over and asked her if there was anyone in the school Andy could speak to.

"Mr. Varano," Andy interrupted, "I'm already talking to a social worker. She's helping me talk through some of the things that I'm dealing with." I was so relieved to hear this. Andy was hurting, but he was doing his very best to heal. I prayed that he would find his way, and I was humbled to have been a small part of his healing process. I'd like Andy to be an example for anyone else who is bullying others.

Whether you're a young student or a middle-aged, unhappy adult harassing people at work, I know you don't really want to be that person.

You know it, too.

It's important for you to understand why you're being

cruel to people. It's not who you were born to be. Somewhere in your life, you were treated unkindly. You had bad things happen to you, or disappointing things, and you are hurting inside. Wouldn't you rather heal that hurt and discover a whole new life, instead of staying trapped in a pit of cruelty and unhappiness? Left unchecked, bullying can escalate to monumentally evil degrees. You see this happening all around the world. Terrorism, for instance, is an extreme version of bullying. Every person who commits these evil acts is filled with rage and misguided frustration. They just have bigger weapons and hurt more people in bigger ways than a typical middle school bully does. It's not okay at that level and it's not okay at any level, whether it's in school or at the workplace - because adults bully, too. They bully people for the same reasons kids bully: they are unhappy. This cycle of bullying needs to be stopped.

I was bullied by coaches. I was bullied by teachers. I was bullied by people I thought were my friends. This made me angry. The anger needed an outlet. So I became the next part of the cycle, and started bullying people, too.

The anger we don't deal with does not go away.

It either destroys us from the inside out, or it becomes the reason we hurt others. When it explodes, it does so in ways that may even confuse us - like in Andy's case. And like in my case, too. I remember being mean to kids. I didn't even know why I was doing it. There was a neighborhood boy I used to play with. At some point I began randomly shoving him down. One minute we'd be playing and the next - BOOM - I'd knock him over for no reason. He was a good kid and never did anything bad to me but there I was doing to him what so many others had done to me.

What was that even about?

I carried the shame of that my entire life.

Then one day years later that boy became my client. He not only forgave me for the bullying I did, he had a conversation with me about it that allowed me to work through all my guilt and shame.

What an extraordinary gift he gave me.

WHAT I CAN CONTROL

AND WHAT I CAN'T

OUT OF MY CONTROL

The past   IN MY CONTROL   What happens around me

The future

My boundaries

My thoughts & actions

The goals I set

What other people think of me

The actions of others

What I give my energy to

How I speak to myself

The outcome of my efforts

The opinions of others

How I handle challenges

How others take care of themselves

infographicdesignby@agrassoblog

Sometimes it will be people we love who bully us.

Maybe they are jealous, or maybe there is some other reason they feel a need to bully us. People bully for many reasons, but it all boils down to feelings of sadness, unhappiness, hurt, and anger. Bullying will escalate if it's not stopped. It will escalate not only for the victim but for the person who is doing the bullying. This is why it matters so much that you speak up and tell someone when you witness a person being bullied. You could actually save a person's life, or prevent them from destroying their own life. You may disrupt the behavior long enough for a person to get help, to heal their heart, and to make better decisions. You may be the catalyst for a bully to get their life together and stay out of prison. You may also prevent a victim from being killed or ending their own life.

Your life is valuable.

You need to tap into the courage it takes to take a stand against being bullied. You need to find the courage to help prevent bullying, or you may always carry the guilt of not doing so.

If you are being bullied, it's important for you to seek help.

Don't just close down and try to get through it on your own. There are people in your life who will help you. There are strangers who will help you. It is critical for you, if you are a child or young adult, to tell an adult - somebody who truly is going to care and help you. And if that person disappoints you by not helping, tell someone else, over and over, as many times as it takes to find help.

It is not okay to live in fear.

I know there are a lot of teachers, coaches, and people in positions of trust, who are not good. Maybe they hate their jobs, or are disenchanted with their own lives, and they don't want to help you.

But on the flip side, so many of these people are amazing and **do** want to help. I always tell students to turn around and look at their teachers in the back of the room. "Guess what their dream was when they were your age?" I ask. "Their dream was to be your teacher. And here you are struggling in school, but you never set up time to go to them after school. You never go and build this relationship with them outside of class. And all they want to do is see you get to the next level."

I know that if students put in the effort to sift through the teachers and adults in their lives, to find the ones who believe in them, it will bring an enormous breakthrough. Too many are out there on their own, using Google and social media to teach themselves about life and self-image. What they really need is interaction with human beings who care about them.

They need people to give them a hug and tell them that they matter.

God did not create a single life that does not matter. Your life is as precious as everyone else's. Do not let yourself become a part of a cycle of bullying that will only bring you down. Do not ever let anyone make you believe you do not have value, or you should not value your own happiness.

You matter.

Key Takeaways from this Chapter:

1. Bullies are suffering from their own emotional pain.

2. It is not okay to live in fear.

3. There is someone in your life who will help you. You may have to sift through some people along the way, but you CAN find someone who will help.

4. You can save a life if you help someone being bullied.

5. You can save a life if you help a bully heal.

6. You matter.

"TO LOVE MEANS LOVING
THE UNLOVABLE. TO FORGIVE
MEANS PARDONING THE UNPARDONABLE.
FAITH MEANS BELIEVING THE
UNBELIEVABLE. HOPE MEANS HOPING
WHEN EVERYTHING SEEMS HOPELESS."
— G.K. CHESTERTON

...KEEP CLIMBING

Chapter Ten
Parents Aren't Perfect

We all want to be the best parents we can be, but parents aren't perfect. There are plenty of resources that will tell you how to be the best parent, but everyone is different. Because of this, it would be impossible to narrow parenting down to one perfect style. Parents were once children, too. How were they raised? What was life like growing up in their childhood homes? Some parents are raised in healthy, encouraging, loving homes. Others are raised in toxic, neglectful, abusive homes. Whether we want to admit it or not, our childhoods affect our parenting styles.

I have known many parents who have come from traumatic childhoods who have become permissive parents; allowing their children to behave in whatever manner they choose, buying them whatever they want, and not correcting them when they are wrong for fear of becoming like their own parents. I have also known many parents who are extremely authoritative, controlling every move their children make, with harsh, unrelenting punishments. And I have also known parents who are loving, involved, and still set boundaries and discipline when needed.

Regardless of how perfect of a parent you try to be, you are still going to make mistakes.

A lot of them.

What I finally realized is that no matter who your parents are, how they raised you, how they championed you, or how they hurt you, I believe the *majority* of all the parents are doing the best they can. However, some parents were never given the tools to be "good" parents. Regardless, most, despite the lack of good examples in their own lives, *want* to be the best they can be.

Sadly though, there are parents who don't fit into this description. Parents who don't try, who put their own needs first, who really don't care about doing what's best. Toxic parents can be neglectful, hurtful or...absent.

At the beginning of my book, I shared how my life began with my father's story. Some of you may be wondering why I didn't mention my mother.

It may take you years to reconcile with a parent, but should that moment arrive, you will be far better served approaching it with an open mind and heart than a closed one.

It took 43 years for me to reconcile with my birth

mother.

When I was two years old, my mother and father bitterly divorced. I was led to believe, that, in retaliation, my mother, Carol, had kidnapped me from my home in New York and brought me to California, in order to hurt my father. Months after the kidnapping occurred, I remember playing on the floor with my train set under the dining room table in my mother's apartment, when my babysitter came in and told me we were going for a ride. Before I knew it, I was in a car with my babysitter and a man I had never met. He was the man my father hired to kidnap me back and we spent the next several days driving back to New York. That was the last time I saw my birth mother.

I was too young to understand what was happening around me. All I knew was one day I lived with both parents. Then it was just my mother, and then my mother disappeared from my life. I had come to the assumption that my mother had only kidnapped me out of spite for my dad, instead of love for me. So there was resentment in my heart, even as I missed her and wondered about her. She was always in the back of my mind and in my heart. In her absence, I missed out on so much. From the time I was two and a half years old until I was 18 years old, I walked through life without anyone to call "Mom."

That changed when my father introduced me to his friend Carole.

At first, I had no idea that Carole had actually been my father's second wife. It didn't strike me as unusual that my father regularly took his young son to a dress shop, either. I just knew we walked in there one day and I met a very special woman.

The Small World Boutique was a dress shop owned by Carole and it was filled with glamorous gowns and cocktail dresses. Neither my dad nor I were shopping for any of that, but the business owner didn't seem to mind. In fact, it seemed like she enjoyed us stopping in as much as we did. I remember how she doted on me. I imagined that's how my mother would have doted on me, if I'd had a real mom.

I remember how friendly she and my dad were to one another. They'd laugh in a way I never saw him laugh with anyone else. I remember thinking how beautiful she was when I met her. Eventually, Carole began coming over for dinner. I loved the nights Karen was there and the four of us spent hours together in the kitchen. We'd make Italian sauce, fresh pasta, and enormous salads while laughing and talking about anything on our minds.

No one was yelling or crying. I wasn't afraid I'd say or do something to set my father off.

It felt like there was nothing but love in the house.

It was an extraordinary time in my life, in a good way, for a change. I was experiencing feelings for Karen that I'd never felt for anyone else and now for Carole, too, in a different, but equally wonderful, way.

About a year after the Sunday Sauce days began, things changed even more.

My father sat Carole and I down together one evening. I sensed something was about to happen and prayed it would not be terrible. I was dumbfounded by what my father said next.

He asked us if we would like to adopt each other.

It sounds strange, right? Asking an 18-year-old boy who is closer to being a man than a child, if he would like to be adopted?

Yet, there is a child inside all of us.

A child who wants to be loved and to give love right back. That child was not buried very far beneath my surface. I knew in that moment what people mean when they say their heart burst with joy, because that's exactly what mine did. It wasn't hard to love Carole. She is an angel in my life. She has been for over 30 years now. Carole helped me learn the business ropes when I opened my portrait studio and she introduced me to the community. Her network became my network, and my business succeeded, in part, because of her.

I love that Carole had the opportunity to meet Lee, too. The night he came to our town and took all of us out for dinner is another special memory I have. My father had never stopped loving Carole. She was his "One That Got Away". I know he was hoping for a second chance with her, but she was already committed to another man. It broke his heart.

I know my father felt the loss at not having another opportunity to be with Carole. He had to live with the consequences of his actions and with the regret. This loss could have been prevented if he'd had the tools he needed to be the husband she deserved. It's hard for me to comprehend how I feel about that possibility, as I would never have been born if my father and Carole had stayed married. So, I just resolved the Lord works in mysterious ways. God knows what we need even when we don't realize it ourselves. He truly loves us even if we don't always believe that.

We are never truly alone.

In our worst moments, when we are in pain, when we feel lost and confused, there are still things being orchestrated for us that we can't see or feel until God reveals them to us.

I'm not sure what went so wrong with my parents that I could not have both of them in my life. Would I have been better off? Maybe.

Or maybe not.

I'll never know. What I do know is that God sent Carole to be in my life, and I am forever grateful. I also know that holding on to resentment towards my father and biological mother, Carol, hurt me. I had to learn to let it go. I just couldn't do that until I went through my life and learned the things I learned, that helped me do so.

One of those teaching moments began with a random message on social media.

"Hey Tom, this is Melanie . . . " the message began.

The only Melanie my mind went to in that moment was a half-sister I'd only heard about. I knew Carol, my biological mother, in the years following the divorce had two more children. One of them was named Melanie.

My heart pounded in my chest. I mean, this is a sister I never met, messaging me out of the blue. It instantly ripped open some wounds I'd been working hard to heal.

"I'd love for you to come up to Canada and have dinner with Mom and I," Melanie wrote.

Reading those words literally froze me in place for several moments. The shock and pain I'd had to navigate my entire life came rushing to the surface, bursting right through the protective walls I'd built. This is it, I thought. My mind flew back to a moment I had with my father when we spoke about my biological mom.

We had gone out for a cup of coffee and some Father-Son time not long after Carole and I adopted one another. "Look, Tom," my father said, "I set this up for you two to have this relationship, but I don't ever want you to forget your biological mother. There may come a time when she comes back into your life."

At the time, I just nodded and agreed. If I were to be honest, I disregarded the entire conversation. But it turned out that my father was right. Even though it was decades later, *that* time, that day had come.

I didn't respond immediately because I needed some time to process her request. Later that night I told Karen about the message. She supported me in whatever my decision would be, like she always does. That made my decision clear.

"I would love to come meet you both," I replied.

We set the meeting up, and I made one more call before I went. I couldn't go meet my biological mother without letting my adoptive mother know. I wanted her to understand that I didn't want to hurt her. You see, years ago, my father and Carole, my adoptive mother, were still married when my father had an affair with my biological mother, Carol. My father broke my adoptive mother's heart. And now here I was, telling her I was going to meet the woman who had played such a large role in her pain.

I was sick to my stomach dialing the phone. But, of course, my adoptive mother showed me that a mother can love a son she didn't give birth to or raise, just as strongly as any other mother. She proved to me once again that she is an angel and I am so, *so* blessed to be loved by her.

"Honey," she said, "people change. Things change. Go and see what she has to say."

And just like that this incredible woman released me from any guilt I felt. She showed me her love for me was so strong, and she trusted in my love for her so strongly, that she wasn't afraid of anyone else taking it away. Not even the same woman who stole her husband's love from her so many years ago.

It was a straight two-hour drive from my town in upstate New York to the Montreal restaurant where our meeting took place. When I arrived, I struggled to keep my nerves at bay. It wasn't hard to pick out my biological mother and my sister; they were the only two customers there. All I could think as they walked toward me was how beautiful they both were. I'm pretty sure I even said that out loud.

My sister hugged me first. When it was Carol's turn, the first thing she said to me was, "I have always loved you."

She wanted to tell me her side of the story. I sat there in that restaurant, feeling like a puzzle being put together piece by piece with my mother's words. All the missing parts of my story were being laid out before me.

This was the first time I learned how hard her life had been with my father. How she was swept up in the things my dad was involved in and how chaotic life had been. Hearing her explain that she'd kidnapped me because she loved me, and didn't want to lose me, had been a puzzle piece I hadn't even been aware was missing. I'd always had that piece marked as Revenge, but really it was Love. She shared her memory of the day my father had kidnapped me back, away from her. How she'd been in the bathroom and I'd been in the dining room. She worked from home so I had a babysitter spending time with me. As my mother talked, I replayed the memory in my own head, lining the two up. It was pretty amazing that I had such a strong memory of that moment, given that I was only two years old. But to this day I can, again, remember playing with my train underneath the dining room table. I remember my babysitter stepping outside to answer a payphone. I remember looking down at her from our second floor window and watching her return to the building.

While my mother was just in the other room, my babysitter scooped me up, along with some of my things, brought me downstairs, and loaded me up in a convertible car that just pulled up out of nowhere. I remember how confused I was and how strange it was to see my babysitter kissing the man who was driving.

I was just a two-year old little boy sitting in the backseat watching one person I barely knew and another I didn't know at all, drive me away from my mother.

Days later, when we rolled up to my father's house, we stepped out of the car and into a party. My father had invited family and friends to welcome me home and everyone was waiting outside. There were balloons and a little remote control car I could sit on and zoom around on. My grandparents were there, too. It was a celebration.

Meanwhile, Carol had been grieving the loss of her son.

It was a bizarre feeling to hear her version of that day as compared to mine. One puzzle piece followed another. Hearing her voice and her laugh - snap! Taking pictures together - snap! Meeting my sister - snap!

By the time I left the restaurant I was feeling newly assembled.

I have a relationship with my biological mom to this day. Not like the one with my adoptive mom, Carole, but we stay in touch. Carole, my adoptive mom, is the one who was in my life from the time I was a young adult through the decades my biological mom missed. She is the one I think of when I hear the word "Mom."

Still, I'm *very* grateful to have this relationship with Carol. I appreciate the heartfelt cards and messages I receive.

I truly believe she loves me.

It took 43 years for me to reconnect with her. She missed my whole life, really. Or at least, enough of it to have missed the opportunity to be the mother I needed. But what I learned from it all is that despite the heartache and havoc that we cause each other, there's always room in the future for reconciliation.

If we're open to believing people can change, then there's a healing that can take place in our lives.

Forgiveness is not always an easy destination. I can't just tell you to forgive your parents. Especially if you have suffered trauma or abuse, which has left a lifetime of scars-physical or emotional. But what I will say is forgiveness is a gift you give to yourself. By forgiving your parents for their mistakes, you're also forgiving yourself for the ones that you may make with your own kids.

Although it's never an easy process, forgiveness is the beginning of the healing process.

It's important to recognize that parents are coming from a place of limitations. You can choose not to let their limitations create limitations within you. Face what has happened in the past. Don't try and bury the pain, or pretend it's not there. Acknowledge all the emotions that come...then let them go.

THIS IS IMPORTANT:

If you're reading this and you are being abused sexually, physically, emotionally, or mentally, then I advise you to seek help. If you are in a dangerous situation it is not okay to just wait it out and hope things will get better because in abusive relationships, most of the time things just escalate.

■■

I want you to know you are not alone.

There are people who can and will help you. It will take courage to seek them out - maybe they are in your school, your workplace, or your church. Maybe they are a family member or maybe an outside resource.

The National Domestic Violence Hotline can also help. Visit their website (https://www.thehotline.org/), or call 1.800.799.SAFE (7233), or text the word START to 88788.

I talk a lot about loving, forgiving, supporting, and showing grace to your parents in this chapter. All of these things are important and meaningful. Sometimes, though, these things come later in life - after you are no longer being abused or neglected by your parents. Sometimes, like me, it will be years later. It is important to be loving, forgiving and supportive to your parents - but not at the expense of your own safety.

Parents aren't perfect.

Key Takeaways from this Chapter:.

1. You can show your parents grace.

2. Comparing our parents to other parents can damage our relationship with them.

3. Parents rise to the highest level they can, with the tools they have. They are not perfect, but most do the best they can with what they have.

4. Your time with your parents is shorter than you think it will be.

5. It takes more courage to look for the good in a parent who lets us down than to focus on the bad.

"DREAMS DON'T WORK
UNLESS YOU DO."
-JOHN C. MAXWELL

...KEEP CLIMBING

Chapter Eleven

Love, Marriage, and Commitment

"Love is a decision, it is a judgment, it is a promise."

Erich Fromm wrote that in his book, *The Art of Loving*. I remembered this quote when I began this chapter, because it is so simple, yet so eloquently true. Love is a decision. It is one we make every day when we decide whether or not we love ourselves, we love our lives, we love one another, or we love God. Love is not a one-and-done kind of thing. If we do not continually reaffirm our commitment to it, it will die.

It seems simple enough, but love can be messy.

Sometimes loving someone or something does not mean we should keep them or it in our lives. Sometimes the greatest act of love we can do for ourselves is to remove a person or a thing from our lives. An abusive spouse or an addictive habit, for instance, are examples of a person or a thing we may love although they hurt us. This can make it very confusing to remove them from our lives, but removing them is something we must do if we want to truly exercise self-love. Sometimes we have to love someone else enough to let them go until they heal themselves. I'm leading with a solemn explanation of love because I want to make it perfectly clear right from the start that your safety is the top priority.

Although love for others is sacred and should be cherished, none of that applies in a situation where any person or habit is hurting you.

I have experienced many kinds of love in my own life: love for my father, my mothers, and family. Love for my wife and children and my friends. Love for God. Love for people I meet along my path. Some of these loves have poured love back over the years. Others have wounded me deeply. Some have done both.

I have grown up in an abusive home.

I have been the child dragged through multiple marriages.

I have been the sibling faced with a terrible decision.

I have been the uncle faced with blinding grief.

I have been the young boy without a real mom.

I have been the young adult drowning in confusion and pain.

Yet, I have also been a young man gifted with the love of a mother who chose to love me, and also the man who reconciled with my biological mother.

I have been the young man gifted with a renewed relationship with a father I loved.

I have been the man blessed with the love of my beautiful, caring wife, who decides she loves me every day.

I have been given the love of two daughters.

I have been shown love from strangers who became mentors and friends.

I have been shown the greatest love of all, the love of God.

All of these experiences have taught me a great many lessons about the power of love. They have shown me the importance of equipping ourselves with the tools to defend and cherish love. They have taught me what those tools are. They have given me firsthand knowledge of the carnage wreaked upon generations when love is given and then taken away. I'm going to share these lessons and this information with you in this chapter, just like I would when I talk to students during my shows. It is so important for all of us to learn more about how to love.

At a school performance, I once asked the Principal what some of the biggest issues were for his students. He thought about that for a while. Then, literally just as I was being introduced by the superintendent, he came running over to me with a revelation.

He told me that the students as young as the fifth grade are having sex in the restrooms and posting suggestive and sexual videos on social media.

This both stunned me and broke my heart.

No 10-year-old child should be making these grown-up decisions about sex, or confusing sex with love. If this is what they learn at such a young age, how are the rest of their lives going to turn out? Will they ever understand what love truly is? Will they ever love themselves enough to protect that special gift? Or will they be like my parents, in and out of relationships and marriages for their whole lives? I am only in these students' lives for a couple of hours. I am not going to be able to really teach them how to end that cycle the way I did in my own life. But I do my very best to plant a seed in their minds and in their hearts, that I hope will one day be allowed to grow. I hope it will grow into minds and hearts that believe love is special. I hope it helps them grow into lives that reflect a respect for their own well-being and the well-being of others.

I hope it will help them avoid the vicious cycle of giving love, only to take it back - and to have it taken back from them. My parents never had anyone plant that seed for them. My parents were married 10 times, between them. I can't imagine the heartache that comes with all those failed marriages. I can't imagine the devastation they must have felt every time their love was accepted and then rejected.

What is it like when you give somebody your heart and then all of a sudden you take it back? What does it do to the way you value marriage, when your marriage dissolves? When you and your husband or you and your wife decide - Hey, I know we said "'til death do we part," but I think we should just forget about that, and walk away.

What happens in a person or in a couple to make them give up on their love? And can it be saved if at least one of them fights for it?

I don't have all the answers to these questions. I hope I never do, really.

I never want to have firsthand knowledge of what it's like to give up on loving my wife, or have her give up on loving me. Not that we haven't had our struggles. It's just that we never gave up on one another. I believe this is both because of our faith and the mindset we had when we got married.

Before I met Karen, I hadn't really believed I would ever be in love. I mean, what was love, really, but an opportunity for heartache and betrayal right? We are all walking this earth with a hole in our hearts. Without faith, we try and fill that hole with things that hurt us or hold us back from realizing our true purpose.

I was probably at my most bitter, jaded place in life when I met Karen. I was 18 and she was 17. I was trying to fill this hollowness inside me with all sorts of bad habits. I dated one girl after another. I was careless with their hearts. I dabbled in recreational drugs and I bought things I didn't need. None of that did anything to help me feel better about my life or myself. If anything, I was growing more depressed and angry. I didn't expect it to be any different meeting Karen than it was to meet any of the other girls I dated.

I've never been so glad to be so wrong.

Karen captivated me from the moment we met. She was so very beautiful. There was an exotic look about her that instantly captured my attention. It did not take long at all for her to capture my heart. Her soft-spoken mannerisms and kindness seemed to close the gaping hollowness inside me a little bit more every minute I was with her.

Our first meeting was a double date. I don't think I even tasted the food. Something strange was happening in my head and in my heart. Something I didn't recognize. I was simply enchanted with Karen.

"I'll call you," I told her as casually as I could when she got out of my car that night.

"No, you won't," she replied flatly, "You don't even have my number."

Never mind that she was right - I didn't have her number . . . yet, but I'd known I'd be calling her long before I dropped her off that night. Getting her number felt like the easy part. A feeling pressed on my heart when we started dating. "Not this one," a voice seemed to be speaking to me. "You're not going to hurt this one."

This was all very confusing territory for me. I didn't really understand what was happening. I just knew that it mattered. I sensed that I was living a moment that could become very important in my life. But was I ready to commit myself to one person? What did I really want out of my life? Did I want to step into a serious relationship? Would I break the cycle I was born and raised in? Was this the time to take that leap?

I really dug deep into myself, asking myself these questions and taking time to think it all through. No matter which way I looked at it, the answer was simple - YES.

That was the best decision of my life.

Karen and I both come from troubled backgrounds.

In fact, the pastor who ran our pre-marital counseling advised us *not* to get married. He was concerned our dysfunctional pasts would hinder our marriage and he believed if we were to marry, it would not last. We were shocked and hurt by his words. But he did not truly see the both of us. Because if he did, he would have recognized the love and commitment we had for one another. If he really knew us he would have recognized the determination we had to not repeat the past. We insisted we wanted to get married. Eventually, he relented, but it was a stressful time for us.

So we had to fight for our marriage even before we were married.

We've fought for it ever since.

I can still close my eyes and see Karen on our wedding day. What made my bride even more beautiful to me was the shared commitment we made privately, before we said our vows in front of God and family.

Divorce would never be an option.

It would never be mentioned, we promised one another.

My father reinforced this committed mindset for me on my wedding day. As Karen and I were preparing to leave our reception, I searched for my father. I couldn't leave without hugging him and saying goodbye. I will never forget what he said to me when I finally found him. Grabbing me by my shoulders, he said, "Son, go. Don't worry about anybody else. You have your own circle now." That line, that quote, always stuck with me. I have my own circle.

My marriage is what I need to focus on and protect above any other relationship.

When you approach a marriage like that, you have no option but to do the work. I believe if everyone made that same commitment far fewer families would know the pain of divorce.

One skill Karen has taught me is communication. It's so important to be able to communicate with one another in a marriage. I tend to be that person who just closes down when I'm hurt. With her help I've learned how to open up to her rather than just shut down. She taught me the importance of commitment and she taught me that love is a verb.

One of my favorite authors, Jim Rohn, wrote "I will take care of me for you. And you take care of you for me." If you walked around with my wife for a month, you would see she does everything possible to take care of herself. Whether it be spiritually, mentally, emotionally, physically; she does all the work in all those different areas. If you are lucky enough to know her, you're amazed by her. Is she perfect? Hardly. She is just as human and fallible as you or I. But flaws are part of what makes us human. Loving one another through our flaws is what matters more.

I hit the jackpot with her.

Yes, we fight.

Yes, we even yell sometimes.

We, as a couple, are no more perfect than we are, as individuals. Our marriage has been tested. I have been tested. One of the first tests involved our church.

After we married, we stayed in the same church for another 10 years. Over time we became uncomfortable with the teachings and a wedge had begun to grow between ourselves and the pastor. As the disconnect grew, it weighed heavily on my wife and I. Karen was the first one to reach her breaking point.

She chose to leave. Yet, I wasn't ready to leave, so I stayed. I can be stubborn sometimes. I can forget the words spoken to me by others and I can drown out the word of God when I forget to listen. One day I was at church, alone, when God spoke to my heart. I heard Him remind me that the pastor is not the person I will be waking up with when I'm 85. It will be Karen. I need to be by her side, not to remain loyal to a pastor who didn't even believe in our marriage. I left that day and I never looked back.

Another test came was when my father passed. The resentment some of my siblings felt toward me was unleashed in full fury. I suppose that resentment had been there all my life. Over time, the lives of some of my siblings became tangled in pain and unhappiness. Eventually, the animosity grew so strong that it impacted my marriage. The hatefulness, the vindictive nature, cruel words and actions became too much. During this tumultuous time, I remembered back to a question Karen had asked long before we married, "Why does your family want to hurt each other all the time? I had no explanation. It took years before I finally recognized how toxic and hurtful my family relations actually were.

This animosity continued for years. It wasn't until the nasty, jealous, backstabbing and toxic ways some of my family dealt with matters that continued to affect my wife and began to affect my children, that I realized I could lose everything I cherished in this world. I was faced with a choice to make. The answer was an easy one, even if the decision was hard to act on. I loved all of my siblings. Family is important to me. I tried everything I could to be a bridge between their resentment and their acceptance. I came to the painful conclusion that I would have to step away from some of my siblings if I wanted to save my marriage and protect my own family from a life of heartache. I knew that unless I made the right decision that *my* own circle be the most important circle in my life, my children and their children would suffer like I did.

I made the decision to break the cycle I was born into.

I put my marriage and my girls above all other relationships.

My parents didn't have the tools and education to remain committed to one another. My father didn't understand back then the words he told me on my own wedding day about the one circle I had to focus on. Maybe at least one of his marriages would have worked if he did. But I am grateful he had the insight to pass on to me, even if it was too late for him to apply in his own life.

Karen and I carry the lessons life has taught us into our marriage. We know when it's time to step back from life and focus on one another. We know how to find resources that help us. There's a book called *The Five Love Languages,* by Dr. Gary Chapman. In it, Dr. Chapman describes the different languages we use to express our love. He teaches us how to translate these languages so we can understand what our spouse is saying, even if their love language is different from ours. It's like having an interpreter in our relationships. I highly recommend it.

Look at love, commitment, and marriage as a recipe.

There are necessary ingredients for this recipe, with selflessness being one of the most important ingredients. Karen is not only a fantastic cook who uses all sorts of recipes to create the most delicious meals I could ask for, she is a phenomenal wife because she follows a recipe for love, marriage, and commitment, and selflessness is one of her main ingredients.

Karen has always put me above her needs. I am nowhere near as good about this as she is, but I am learning how to be better about it. If you are expecting your husband or wife to save you from your problems, to "fix" everything for you, you are missing a key ingredient of love, marriage, and commitment. It will never work.

Your spouse is not your savior. God is.

If, however, you enter marriage with a commitment to truly love and serve your spouse, putting him or her above your own needs, you are on a winning path. Of course, this requires both of you to have the same mindset. Maybe a marriage can last with only one person doing the work, but it will most likely not be a happy marriage. The person doing all the giving, all the work, will be sacrificing their happiness for the sake of their spouse. That's a tragedy. When both partners commit to serving one another - a marriage truly flourishes. If I put Karen's needs above mine and she puts my needs above hers, our marriage lives in a space of selflessness. We both see and appreciate what the other one does for us. We are both inspired to do more for one another. That puts us in a position of strength when adversity comes knocking.

Selflessness is absolutely a critical ingredient for a strong marriage, but it is not the most important one. In my marriage, commitment to put God above all else is the true tie that binds. It may sound like putting God above my wife is unfair to my wife, but hear me out. We both made a decision to put God first.

Our marriage is like a triangle, with God at the top.

As we learn and grow in God, we become closer together. In essence, it makes us closer. We are rooted in the love that He truly wants us to have. As we both subconsciously chart our paths toward a relationship with Christ, we inevitably fulfill our vows to one another.

If someone like me can find love and a fulfilling marriage, anyone can. No matter what story you are born into, you are your own author in life. With all the heartache I was born into and all the trauma I have experienced, I could very well have been stuck in the pit of life, repeating the same cycle of unhappiness. Karen and I could have let our pastor's prognosis of failure convince us not to get married. We could have walked away from one another and fulfilled his expectations that neither of us would ever have the tools to be in a loving, lasting marriage but we didn't and you don't have to let anyone else convince you that you are not good enough for love, either.

There is plenty of hope for you to have a strong marriage. You just have to see how special and important it is. You have to be ready to prioritize it above all other relationships in your life. You have to understand that you are not doomed to live in the cycle you were born into. Conversely, if you are blessed with parents who are in a loving, lasting marriage, you will only experience the same results if you learn from their example.

You will have your heart broken in this life. You will face pain and struggle. But you do not have to face it alone. In fact, you are not facing it alone. God is always with you, even if you don't believe that is the case. God will send opportunities for love into your life. It will be up to you to recognize those opportunities. It will be up to you to cherish the heart of a person who gives you their love, and to defend that love against all who seek to come between it.

I wish for you the kind of love I have with my wife.

I wish for you to have and to be for someone else, the person she is for me.

She makes me better in all the areas of my life. She forces me to be better. When you have people in your life like that, whether it be friends, family, or your spouse, you've hit the

jackpot, too.

Key Takeaways from this Chapter:

1. You can break generational cycles of heartache.

2. You are never truly alone.

3. Love may start out as a feeling but it can only last as a commitment.

4. Your marriage is your most important human relationship in life.

5. Selflessness is a key ingredient in the recipe for a strong marriage.

"A HERO IS AN ORDINARY INDIVIDUAL WHO FINDS THE STRENGTH TO PERSEVERE AND ENDURE IN SPITE OF OVERWHELMING OBSTACLES."

-CHRISTOPHER REEVE

...KEEP CLIMBING

Chapter Twelve
It's Not a Miracle

One of my favorite movies is *Apollo 13,* starring Tom
Hanks. In this movie, Tom-portrays a character named Jim
Lovell. The first scene opens up with the Lovells having a house
party to celebrate the live footage of the first moonwalk. After
the party ends Jim is sitting in the backyard, looking up at the
night sky and the moon. When his wife, Marilyn, sits next to
him, Jim holds his thumb up framing the full moon, then turns
to her and says, "From now on, we live in a world where man has
walked on the moon. It's not a miracle, we just decided to go."

Something about those words strikes a chord in me. It
resonates with me on so many levels. I use this quote in my
shows, fitting it in different places depending on the portraits I
am painting. If I am painting a soldier, a law enforcement officer,
or a first responder, I talk about how they choose to go into
danger so that they may rescue or defend others.

I use this quote when I talk about key figures in this life
who have inspired us and changed this world. Saint Teresa of
Calcutta, for instance, chose to spend her life helping others

discover the gifts of love and compassion. She sought out the most unloved, uncelebrated people in the world to give her love to. She offered aid and comfort to those suffering around her. She wrapped her arms around them and helped them find the care they deserved. Even if that care couldn't save them, even if it just meant they were given dignity in their last moments on this earth, Saint Teresa made sure those days were filled with the kind of love and kindness those afflicted people had never seen.

Saint Theresa has been known to intercede in miraculous ways, but her actions, her choice, to enter into poverty so that she might serve the poor was not. She prayed, listened to God, and CHOSE to go. She chose to forsake all her material possessions and devote her entire existence to serving and caring for others.

She lived one of the most unselfish lives anyone has ever lived.

That was her dream and she lived it.

Another person whose portrait I often paint and whose story I talk about during my shows is Nelson Mandela. He spent over 9,000 days in prison for his dream of ending apartheid. He spent a total of 27 years in prison. He was in his seventies when he was released from this bondage. He could have chosen to spend the rest of his days trying to live a peaceful life. But Nelson chose to run for the office of the president of South Africa - and he won. That wasn't a miracle. Nelson chose to overcome his cruel captivity. He chose to forgive. He chose to remain committed to a cause. He chose to step forward and serve - to be the example of leadership.

Michael Jordan is another favorite of mine. He was cut from his high school basketball team. He could have quit right there. He could have given up on his dream.

But Michael Jordan chose to be his own miracle.

He chose to dig deep, to dedicate himself to the sport he loves, to humble himself to acknowledge he wasn't yet good enough, but determined to be better; to believe in himself enough to push through years of struggle, to overcome the odds and step into life as a legend. Michael Jordan proved to us all that it can be done.

The human spirit is powerful.

When we tap into it, we can accomplish things bigger than our minds tell us are possible.

We don't have to become world famous like Saint Teresa or Michael Jordan. We don't have to literally be canonized as a saint, or hailed as among the greatest of all time for some skill or talent we possess, to be a miracle in our own lives and an inspiration to others. We can be "everyday" people like me, or like Dave Massett.

I met Dave when I was a teenager. Another epic movie had come out. The moment I saw *Top Gun*, I was convinced I wanted to be a Navy pilot. This was my first experience with true inspiration. It was my first taste of having a real dream, a real vision for what my life could be like one day. I was obsessed. I started learning all about the Navy, planes, and ships. We did not have a lot of money, but somehow my father found a way to pay for me to take flying lessons. I was just a teenager, the same age we all are when we first get our driver's licenses, and here I was learning how to fly a plane. What an experience!

The Oneida County Airport had two runways positioned on 1,800 acres. It was just a small county airport but to me it was paradise. Dave Massett was the training pilot. He was an amazing teacher.

Dave was in his twenties. Everything about him screamed of a love for flying. You know when you are with someone and you can see the passion they have for what they are doing? That was Dave. His dream was to become a commercial airline pilot. His job as a pilot instructor not only helped him earn an income, it gave him the chance to put in the flight time needed to move into that field.

Dave was a perfect teacher for me. It was a privilege to be trained by someone who loved what he was doing so much and understood my passion for it.

Up in the air with Dave, everything else melted away.

I wasn't a kid feeling lost without a mom.

I wasn't exhausted from the constant volatility in my home.

I wasn't the struggling student with ADHD and a growing chip on my shoulder.

I wasn't betrayed by people I trusted.

I wasn't any of that.

I was Tom Varano, pilot in training. I was limitless. I was in the clouds and weaving through sunbeams. I looked down upon my town that felt like a prison at times, and I saw for miles beyond it. I saw how small it was. I saw my future.

I loved every single minute of the 90-minute trainings. From the coursework to the flying time, it was not just an escape - it was a map to the rest of my life. We flew in a little Cessna 152-single prop plane. The pre-checks are something that can absolutely never be skipped. If there was a problem with any inch of the plane, you want to know that *before* you are thousands of feet in the air, or speeding down a runway. I loved learning how to check the fuel, the propeller, and how to go through all these different steps to make sure our plane was in top shape for our flight.

One of the most intense lessons I had was the instrument training. This means that I was taught to fly without looking out the plane windows for a visual. I could only use my instruments and the readings on them, to pilot the plane. To make sure I couldn't cheat - even just out of a panic or instinct - a helmet was placed on my head. It blocked every line of sight except the instruments. It may seem extreme and scary but it had a purpose - imagine flying through a sudden storm or fog, or being faced with an emergency landing, where there are no ground lights, and no visibility in the air, for you to see a mountain or a telephone wire or even the ground? If you do not know how to immediately read and process the instruments in your plane, you will crash. It's as simple as that.

It's also not the scariest training there is. I'm speaking of the emergency stall. What's that, you ask? Well, it's pretty much exactly what it sounds like. You know what happens when your car stalls? How it sort of either silently and swiftly just shuts off, or it may buck for a minute and then shut off? If you're lucky, it happens in a driveway or on a quiet road where you can safely exit the vehicle or try to restart it.

Now imagine flying a plane when it stalls.

There is no safe place to pull over for a minute. There are only a few precious seconds to restart the engine or figure out how to land with no power or to eject in some instances, before you die. It is not something you want to experience without the confidence and training to block everything else out, especially fear.

Air traffic control must approve all flight plans before anyone takes to the sky. Without this, there would be no order. It would be total chaos with massive casualties. Each pilot is given coordinates and a lane to stay in for every leg of their flight. Dave had already cleared this emergency stall training. He'd been given the coordinates and ample open air to do so.

Up we went, all the way to 10,000 feet. Dave sat back from his controls while I used mine to fly the plane, like he always did. It takes a special kind of confidence to be Dave in this moment.

We hit the specified altitude and he killed the engine.

The plane dove. Fast. I was 16 years old and used to driving within 25-55 mph speed limits on the ground - even though I had only just begun to drive. Suddenly I was hurling hundreds of miles an hour towards the ground from an altitude of 10,000 feet.

Terrifying does not even begin to describe this experience.

With no engine running, the only sounds louder than the wind rushing against the plane were my heart slamming frantically against my chest, and the petrified screams in my head. In between those sounds, it was possible to hear the creaks of the plane. It's an eerie feeling. You're diving faster and faster and you quickly get to a point of no return. This is the point where it's not possible for a pilot to pull out of a dive. A plane is heavy. It doesn't just reverse gravity on a dime at hundreds of miles an hour.

If you've ever been in a situation that was so terrifying you felt paralyzed with fear, you know what I'm talking about here. If not, there's a good chance you will be in one someday, so you'll want to train yourself for it.

In the thousands of hours that pilots train, they learn how to step back out of a situation, find calmness, and work the problem. This same technique can be applied to other professions and in all our lives.

The human spirit is really remarkable that way. I recently saw an article about a female pilot with 150 passengers on board her plane. When one of the plane's engines died, she was able to tap into her training and remain calm to work the problem. She saved 150 people and their families who love them, because she chose to commit herself to that training.

Whatever the problem we are faced with, removing our emotions in order to remain calm and tap into our training is key.

If we allow emotions to kick in, we do not think clearly enough to work the problem. This holds true in relationship conflict, work conflict, and everyday life. This is what makes certain athletes so phenomenal. That's why Michael Jordan was given the ball in the last seconds of the game, because everyone knew he would remain calm and make that winning shot more often than he would miss.

Dave mastered this skill, himself. He just calmly talked me through the lesson. His voice remained soothing and his advice simple: "Stick to what you learned. Remember what we've gone over."

It made all the difference in the world. I was able to push panic away and think clearly. I had to resolve the situation. I had to work the problem. And I did.

Our lives can feel like this sometimes. Like we are in a free fall to disaster and we either work the problem or we allow the problem to destroy us. Panic has no place in those moments. We can let all those emotions hit us later - *after* the problem has been solved. But in the moment, it is the training we've had that will determine the outcome: Will we be calm and in command of our actions? Will we rise to the occasion and be our own miracle - and maybe someone else's? Or have we not learned how to believe in ourselves and in God's guiding grace to the point that we can channel our will and our minds to survive and thrive?

Dave was an excellent teacher. He had prepared me well for this moment. I was able to restart the plane and pull it up out of the dive. If Dave was panicking at all he didn't let me see it. Or maybe my own adrenaline rush overpowered everything else.

It was one of the most exhilarating moments of my life.

In a way, I try to help my audiences pull out of their own nose dives every time I am on stage. I may not know what challenge is stalling their spirit and tilting them towards a deadly dive, but I know many of them are in that battle for their happiness and well-being. I know that they will face those moments throughout their lives, and if I can help just one person through planting a seed of resilience or faith that they can nurture for those times, it is worth it. If I can help just one person muster the courage to continue battling the need to bully others, it is worth it. If I can disrupt a pattern of hopelessness and depression for someone, long enough for them to restart their own spiritual engine and pull out of a nose-dive, it is worth it.

Sadly, I never pursued my dream of becoming a Navy pilot. All it took for me to give up on my dream was the opinion of an assistant coach in high school. I still remember his sneer when he looked at me and told me I'd never make it. I knew he didn't like me, but I let him convince me that was true.

Unfortunately the same year I was studying to become a pilot my family suffered a house fire. We were forced to move into a hotel and my father's financial situation changed. He was unable to pay for the completion of my certification and I never got to fly with Dave again.

Until years later when I stepped onto a plane for a flight, heading to NYC to visit Lee one day. I took one look at the Captain greeting his passengers and stopped dead in my tracks.

It was Dave.

We locked eyes and started laughing. "Dave, Dave you did it!" I was bursting with happiness as I passionately shook his hand and congratulated him. His smile was as big as mine. It was an amazing, special moment I will never forget.

Dave's story is your story. It's my story.

It's the story we can all write for ourselves. He didn't sit back and wait for a miracle to fall into his lap, that would gift him his dream of being a commercial airline pilot. He chose to work for it. He chose to pour just as much passion into teaching a 16-year-old boy how to fly, as he put toward his own dream.

There are times I feel a wave of nerves before I go on stage. It's more than a performance for me. I feel just as much responsibility to come through for my audiences as Dave Massett must have felt to bring us both through our lessons safely. I think about taking them up and out of their lives for a moment, to help them feel just the way I did when I was flying with Dave.

Years ago, I had the opportunity to perform at a school where two of my very own former high school teachers were working. There was a part of me that wanted them to see what the "problem" student had become; a man living his dream.

But after the show, I received quite a surprise. I was doing the meet and greet with students who were lined up to talk with me and I nearly fell over when one of them shook my hand and told me I knew his dad - Dave Massett. He passed along his father's sentiments, telling me how much he loved what I was doing.

It was one more emotional moment in my life. But it wasn't a miracle at all, was it?

Rather, it was the culmination of two men choosing to go after their dreams, and how our paths intertwined for a handful of heartbeats. We touched each other's lives in meaningful ways neither of us will ever forget.

You have moments like that before you, waiting for you to choose to live them.

Today is the perfect day to start asking yourself the questions, that will lead you there:

What is it that you want to do?

What do you want your life to look like in the future?

What gets you excited?

What's on the top shelf in your life, that you don't have the resources for right now, but you dream of?

Maybe it's a home. Maybe it's a beautiful car. Maybe it's

money in your pocket to give away, whatever it is, those are your dreams. I don't know what those things are, but they're on that imaginary top shelf. And those are the things that you want out of this life.

So what are you going to do to focus your life, to be able to reach some of those dreams?

Nobody else can tell you what you need to do with your life. People may want to make suggestions because they love you and believe they know what's best for you. You may hear them tell you how you "should" do this or you "should" do that. That's all great. But those people who are suggesting those things don't have to do the work. They don't have your dreams in their hearts. They don't have to live with the consequences of your decisions. You do.

Whatever it is you choose to do, you have to love it. Without a passion and love for the path you are pursuing, you will not have the tenacity to see it through. You will not be a sponge, soaking up every morsel of information on the subject. You will not be willing to push through the hard times that separate those who quit from those who do not.

Saint Teresa became a professional lover of people. Michael Jordan became a professional basketball player. Dave

Massett became a professional airline captain.

What will you choose to become?

I can sometimes feel overwhelmed when I am in front of thousands of students. Recently I broke down on stage, looking at the faces of the students who were leaning forward, eagerly listening to what I had to say and I could see they were feeling the emotions with me. And they got it.

These students came up to me, crying because they wanted to change, but they just didn't know how. They're not being encouraged enough. They aren't being given the training to believe in themselves and to make the decisions that lead them to their dreams.

It breaks my heart because I know what it's like to be just like them, to be stuck in that pit wanting desperately to escape. To feel like there is no escape. And I also know that we all have the ability to do incredible things with our lives.

You have the ability to do incredible things with your life.

All you have to do is choose to go.

• •

On the stage, I love beginning each portrait upside down, feeling the audience attempting to figure out what I'm doing and feeling the wonder with them each time I flip it right side up. They are wholly invested in me in those moments, listening to the specific music or soundtrack accompanying each portrait I paint. Although I've done it thousands of times, the moment I cover my hand in paint, lift it high, and place my handprint on the completed portrait, a wave of emotion covers me.

I love sensing the audience's emotions when I flip the painting right side up and see the power of that simple flip; when they realize the power they have to completely flip their own realities and change their lives for the better.

Key Takeaways from this Chapter:

1. We all have the ability to do great things with our lives.

2. When faced with a crisis or a challenge, remember to work the problem, not your emotions.

3. Faith & Passion will be the fuel to get you through the hard times.

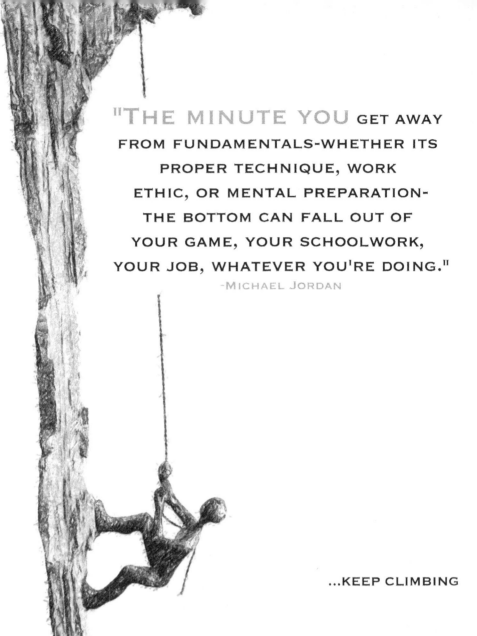

"THE MINUTE YOU GET AWAY FROM FUNDAMENTALS-WHETHER ITS PROPER TECHNIQUE, WORK ETHIC, OR MENTAL PREPARATION- THE BOTTOM CAN FALL OUT OF YOUR GAME, YOUR SCHOOLWORK, YOUR JOB, WHATEVER YOU'RE DOING."
-MICHAEL JORDAN

...KEEP CLIMBING

Epilogue

Congratulations on completing this journey with me. Now, as you close this book, take the lessons you have learned and let them inspire you. Remember that life's obstacles are not meant to define us but to shape us into the best versions of ourselves. The stories you have encountered within these pages serve as a testament to the human capacity for resilience, courage, and unwavering hope.

As you continue your own journey, know that you, too, possess the strength to overcome any obstacle that may come your way. You have witnessed firsthand the power of determination, perseverance, and the belief in one's own abilities. You have read about wins and losses. No matter how difficult the road ahead may seem, you have seen that it is possible to rise above the challenges and forge a path towards success and fulfillment.

May the stories within this book serve as a guiding light, reminding you that you are capable of achieving greatness, no matter the odds stacked against you.

Embrace the lessons learned and let them fuel your own pursuit of a life filled with purpose, resilience, and the unwavering belief in your own potential.

As you turn the final page, carry with you the knowledge that you are the author of your own story. Embrace the challenges, celebrate the victories, and let the journey unfold with determination, courage, and unwavering faith in the incredible strength that lies within you.

Your next chapter awaits, and I believe the odds are forever in your favor. May God's grace, peace and blessings be with you on your journey.

Tom

TO LEARN MORE ABOUT:

-BOOKING TOM FOR NATIONAL LIVE SPEED
PAINTING/SPEAKING EVENTS-INCLUDING K-12
SCHOOLS, COLLEGES, CHARITY AND CORPORATE EVENTS.

-PURCHASING COMMISIONED ART

-PURCHASING ADDITIONAL BOOK COPIES
AND OTHER MERCHANDISE

-DONATING TOWARDS OUR MISSION IN K-12 SCHOOLS

PLEASE VISIT OUR WEBSITE AT:
WWW.EMOTIONINTOART.COM
TOM@VARANO.COM
INSTAGRAM.COM/TOMVARANO

EMOTION
—INTO—
ART

K-12 SCHOOLS-COLLEGES-CHARITIES-CORPORATE

WOULD YOU BE SO KIND AFTER READING THIS BOOK
TO LEAVE ME AN HONEST AMAZON REVIEW.
THANK YOU!

Made in the USA
Monee, IL
12 August 2023